Through the Eyes of Cleopas

Thru The First Disciple's Eyes, Volume 3

John H Brennan

Published by John H Brennan, 2023.

THROUGH THE EYES OF CLEOPAS

First edition. June 22, 2023.

ISBN: 979-8223723912

Written by John H Brennan.

To my beloved brothers in Christ, Raymond Rodrigues-Torres and his brother Ralph Rodrigues-Torres and in memory of Ray and Shannah's daughter Bella who will always remain in my heart until she sits on my lap in eternity as she introduces me to Mommy Church.

Introduction

Fifteen years ago, I was invited to an "Emmaus" retreat. My best friend, Raymond, lives in Miami and his brother, Ralph lived in Orlando. Ray gave me two choices; it was either his retreat thru Saint John Neumann's Catholic Church in Miami in six weeks from then or it was at his Ralph's retreat at Holy Family Church in Orlando a couple months after that. There was no third option.

God tends to do that as well – puts you at a fork in the road where one direction is the one He wants you to take, the other direction is different – the pavement stops a mile away, but up ahead you see pavement ahead. The area between the paved sections seems solid enough to drive on, so you slowly drive off the pavement and someone flies by you in a off road vehicle, but they don't go on toward the pavement, they begin their off-road journey. You stop the car, get out and look around. You have no idea where the other vehicle went, but they sure did look like they were having fun.

You are tempted to follow the path, as your vehicle also is 4-wheel drive. Anywhere they can go, I can too, right? But after a few feet, you realize that the sand there is dry and would be easy for you to get stuck. So you back up, and head for the pavement. You realize the paved road loops back and rejoins the original other choice. Why did this happen?

It doesn't take a genius to figure out that God is watching over you. Not to gather a laundry list of little things when you made a bad choice, but to offer you many opportunities to return to the right choice. He lets us make these bad choices because He wants us to be free – free to choose right or wrong but always seems to be there to help you pick up the broken pieces of our life, until we run out of time in this life.

I ended up going to the Orlando Emmaus Retreat. It was an awesome experience I never will forget. It's a great spiritual model to recognize that we never walk alone. You may be Cleopas or you may be the unnamed disciple, but Jesus will join you in your moments of despair and disappointment. The encounter with Jesus on the road to Emmaus in Luke's Gospel is so deep in love. Not surprising when you think about it, Jesus is in it!

Always remember, it starts with two people walking. Are they walking away from something or toward something? When they left Jerusalem for Emmaus, were they confident enough with the stories that Jesus had risen and wanted to take the two hour walk home to share the news with their neighbors in the little town of Emmaus?

Or were they disappointed that His Body was stolen and hope has faded? Did Luke forget the name of the other disciple who traveled with Cleopas or did he purposely allow us be able to, 2000 years later, place ourselves in that spot to console Cleopas? Do we have moments where we feel like we are unnamed?

There are no right or wrong answers, as in this particular corner of the jigsaw puzzle of Scripture. The piece in your hand that not only fits in the spot also will complete the picture. Why? Because God enabled you to pick up that one puzzle piece when He knows He needs you to complete the picture.

His plan is a wonderful Plan. He knows each of us because since the beginning of time He knew you would be right to live today and would be receptive to the call He has for you! He knows that you don't mind being either Cleopas today or the unnamed disciple! In either role, He knows that you have a shoulder to lean on, to cry over or you know how to use the shoulder of the named one who may be stronger, spiritually, emotionally or physically. His wonderful plan also recognizes there are times when two or more are together, they may be wandering on the path and need Him to walk along side of them to guide them back.

Unlike Cleopas, I will not share my walk details with you, but since my retreat in Orlando, I brought my oldest son John to Raymond's retreat in Miami as I followed the retreat leader, Jorge, behind the scenes of a big men's retreat. It is so great to be the unnamed disciple in this case, having no apparent role, but to observe and do what I was asked when there was a need. My son Andy also has attended an Emmaus Retreat, this one in Pittsburgh, Pa. Where I have many true brothers in Christ whose desire to be humble will be here "The other disciple".

So, when, in Luke's Gospel, Cleopas and the other disciple met up, unknowingly, with Jesus on the road to Emmaus and He opened up the scriptures to them, what did they discuss in this seven-mile walk? Everything is possible with God, but Luke doesn't describe a lightning bolt hitting them infused with Scripture, so what would Jesus have done with this two-hour talk?

You will see in this book what I believe they did and talked about. Remember that God always was and always will be. He is all knowing and all loving. He is the author of all life. The enemy, satan, only knows what he sees and hears. He is a great observer of what we do and where our weaknesses are. He seeks a crack in the foundation of our life.

Owning a home with a basement allows you to see this concept very clearly. One thinks the concrete blocks or poured concrete form a good, solid foundation. Of course, we allow dirt to be piled up on the outside and sometimes you get too busy with life and it rains and rains and rains. Low spots form under those beautiful bushes where you don't notice the rain tunneling it's way to the outside of the concrete. Repeated early freezes and then thaws (in my upstate NY neighborhood) begin a crack.

There is something about wetness that multiplies crack propagation and before you know it, you have puddles on your basement floor in the spring when it rains. This is exactly how the evil one works in our lives. He is slow and methodical. He looks for the homes with no or careless landscaping – where the dirt invites the rain to follow the slope down toward the weak structure. He doesn't bother with the ones with proper drainage away from the house.

The evil one can't see the future; he can only see the patterns of the past and guess his next move. But God is not bound by time. He knows what mistake we are about to make and changes the scenario somehow to preserve our freedom to choose the wrong path, but will take delight if we choose the right path!

When He died on the cross, the evil one believes he won. He got all the chief priests, Judas, and many others to choose the path to kill Jesus, but Jesus chose to come here on Earth at that specific time knowing that many people went to sleep asking for forgiveness for allowing evil into their lives and needed forgiveness. He knew that I would choose evil yesterday, maybe weeks ago also, maybe years ago, and needed to know that I could be released from the bondage of sin and that the fear of death would be replaced with the joy of death, knowing that God loved me so much, He sent His only Son to die a sacrificial death to erase the stain of sins repented.

I believe that Jesus made the following items from Scripture very understandable to Cleopas and the other disciple:

- **The Incarnation:** Jesus is the Son of God who took on human form. By becoming fully human while remaining fully divine, Jesus entered into the brokenness of the world to offer salvation and redemption. This act challenged the power of evil and darkness.
- **Temptation and Victory:** Prior to His public ministry, Jesus experienced temptation in the wilderness, where the devil attempted to exploit His vulnerability. However, Jesus resisted the temptations and emerged victorious,

demonstrating His power over evil.

- **Teaching and Miracles**: Throughout His ministry, Jesus taught about God's kingdom, emphasizing love, compassion, and forgiveness. He performed miracles, healing the sick, casting out demons, and even raising the dead. These acts demonstrated God's power over evil and brought hope to those who were suffering.
- **Crucifixion and Resurrection**: Jesus' crucifixion and subsequent resurrection are central to the Christian faith. Although the crucifixion appeared to be a victory for evil, it ultimately led to the defeat of death and sin. Jesus' resurrection showed His triumph over evil and opened the way for eternal life for all who believe in Him.

Specific details about Jesus' movements leading up to His crucifixion, such as going to Bethany, Jericho, back to Bethany and then to Jerusalem, riding into Jerusalem on a donkey, all immensely hold symbolic significance in Christian tradition as well as gives people the opportunity to choose sides as well as taunts the evil one. I can only imagine how satan sees them prepare to go to Jerusalem, then goes way off course to Jericho. Ah, Jesus must be nervous; maybe he doesn't want to die for those sinful people after all!

Then He leaves Jericho and ends up back in Bethany! Satan must have really loved that he was so close to winning! Then he sees Jesus riding into Jerusalem on a donkey, which is often seen as a fulfillment of prophecy and a representation of humility and peace, but he knows that the Chief Priests were already jealous about Jesus – and now he declares himself a king! We got him now, right? But Jesus has this all planned. He let the evil ones who continue to desire evil to continue to do evil to complete his objectives, not the objectives of the evil one.

In His omniscience and love, God has a plan to counter the schemes of all evil and bring about redemption. Through Jesus' life, death, and resurrection, the power of evil is ultimately overcome, and humanity is offered the opportunity to choose the path of goodness, love, and salvation.

Yes, if you are, or want to become people of faith, believe that God continues to work in the world today. He continues guiding and intervening in various ways to counteract the plans of evil. Perceive these instances as "God-Incidences" or divine interventions, where seemingly coincidental events align to produce positive outcomes or prevent potential harm.

The belief in God's providence and His involvement in human affairs is deeply rooted in religious traditions, but is obvious to those who accept God. While individuals may interpret and experience these interventions differently, many find comfort and affirmation in perceiving these events as signs of God's presence and care.

All we have to do is to know that He is guiding researchers to discover cures for diseases or orchestrating timely interventions to prevent accidents. Believe in divine guidance and providence! These occurrences are often seen as evidence of God's love, protection, and desire to bring about good in the world.

Ultimately, when we take our last breath, we will know if we were walking with an unnamed disciple sharing our sorrows when Jesus walked up out of nowhere and showed us that we were worthy of His Love or if it was just a guy were hang out with and a stranger who wanted a ride 7 miles down the road and we all went our merry ways when we got there.

Cleopas Receives Messenger from Solomon's Portico

Mary, my love, gather close and listen to what I have to share. Just moments ago, a messenger arrived with tidings that stirred my soul to its core. He informed me that our nephew, Jesus, is up in Jerusalem, in Solomon's Portico. But that's not all, my dear; the news he brought carried a weight of fear and concern.

You remember, don't you? A short time after my brother Joseph passed away, his son, Jesus, went through an extraordinary journey. He was baptized by John in the River Jordan, and then, led by the Spirit, he ventured into the desolate wilderness to pray and fast for forty days.

Oh, the trials he faced during those forty days! The evil one, in his wickedness, tried to tempt Jesus' time and again. I can't forget that final temptation, when the devil carried Jesus to the top of the temple tower, whispering in his ear to worship him in exchange for all the kingdoms of the world.

Now, in the same place, the tables are turned. Many know who Jesus is and what He is capable of. The evil one also knows and his back is against the wall. So like the evil demons flew into the swine, the evil one flew into the Jews in the Portico. But instead of doing line they did in the swine, this time they try to manipulate the Jewish leaders into a jealous rage and want to stone Jesus. But he just walked away, without a scratch. He stood strong, firm in his conviction, and rebuked the devil, declaring that it is the Lord God whom we should worship alone. The enemy fled, defeated by the indomitable spirit of Jesus. The lines were drawn in the sand and the war was kicked into high gear.

And now, Mary, I sense a shift in the air, a change that whispers of something momentous about to unfold. The messenger spoke of Jews in Jerusalem, accusing Jesus of blasphemy. They wish to stone him Mary. Can you fathom such hatred?

It leads me to believe that Jesus is about to make his move, to fulfill his divine purpose. The trials he endured in the wilderness, the temptations he faced—perhaps they were preparing him for this very moment. I see a fire in his eyes, a determination that burns brighter than ever before.

My heart swells with both pride and concern Mary. Pride for the extraordinary man our family has raised, the one destined to change the world, and concern for the dangers that surround him. We must keep him in our thoughts, our prayers, and trust that God's hand guides him through this treacherous path.

I know it won't be easy, my dear. But together, as a family, we will support Jesus with unwavering love. We shall be his strength when he feels weak, his refuge in the storm. Let us hold on to hope, for it is hope that keeps us going, even in the darkest of times.

So, Mary, my love, let us remain steadfast in our faith. Let us keep our hearts open and trust that the path our dear Jesus walks is one destined for greatness. May God protect him and guide him, for he carries the weight of the world upon his shoulders.

Of course, my dear Mary. Let me continue with the narrative.

As I stand here before you, recounting these events, my mind races with memories of the miracles Jesus performed. The blind received their sight, the lame walked, and the deaf heard the melodies of life once again. The compassion and love that radiated from him were unlike anything I had ever witnessed.

But with such power comes great responsibility, and I fear that those who oppose Jesus, who see him as a threat, will stop at nothing to silence his voice. Yet, I refuse to let fear consume me, for I have seen the light that shines within him.

As I spoke with the messenger, his words echoed in my ears. Many Jews in Jerusalem believed Jesus had blasphemed, but I know the truth, Mary. I know that his teachings are born of divine wisdom, his actions guided by a love beyond comprehension.

We must be prepared for what lies ahead. Let us gather our strength, our courage, and be ready to face whatever challenges arise. I trust that Jesus will not falter in the face of adversity, that he will stand tall against the stones thrown in his path.

Oh, Mary, my heart aches for our beloved nephew. But I also feel a sense of hope, a glimmer of anticipation that dances within me. I believe that Jesus is on the precipice of something extraordinary, something that will change the course of history forever.

In these uncertain times, let our love for Jesus be a beacon of light, guiding us through the darkness. Let us hold on to faith, for it is faith that sustains us, that reminds us of the miracles we have already witnessed.

We will face trials and tribulations Mary, but we will face them together. Our unwavering love and unyielding support shall be a shield for Jesus, a sanctuary amidst the storm. Let us pray for his safety and well-being, knowing that our prayers reach the ears of the Almighty.

Mary, as I look into your eyes, I see a reflection of my own hopes and fears. We have been blessed with a nephew who possesses a strength and grace beyond measure. And though the path before him may be treacherous, I know that he is destined for greatness.

So, let us gather our thoughts, our prayers, and hold on to the faith that has carried us through countless trials. The message has been delivered; the warning received. Now, let us be prepared for the next chapter in the extraordinary journey of Jesus, our nephew, our hope, and our guiding light.

Together, Mary, let us embrace the unknown with open hearts, for our love will carry us through, no matter what lies ahead.

The Lamb of God in Bethabara Again?

Honey, you won't believe the news that reached my ears. It was a day filled with revelations and a sense of anticipation. I learned that our nephew Jesus, was spotted on his way to Bethabara, the very place where John the Baptizer called him the "Lamb of God" for the first time. The implications of such a momentous encounter are staggering.

As the words reached me, a wave of memories flooded my mind. I recalled when John told me, with conviction in his voice, said he pointed towards Jesus and declared him as the Lamb of God. It was a proclamation that reverberated in our souls, filling us with a profound sense of awe and wonder. We knew then that something extraordinary was unfolding before our eyes.

Now, as we stand on the pinnacle of this new revelation, I can't help but speculate about what lies ahead for Jesus. The title "Lamb of God" carries immense significance, symbolizing sacrifice, redemption, and a divine mission.

Could this mean that Jesus is about to embark on a path that leads to the fulfillment of his purpose? Is he preparing to embrace his role as the sacrificial lamb, the one who will carry the burden of humanity's sins? The weight of such a calling is both humbling and awe-inspiring.

I can't help but wonder if Jesus, in his infinite wisdom, is now stepping into a new phase of his ministry. The time for miracles, teachings, and transformative acts may be drawing to a close, making way for the ultimate sacrifice that will shape the destiny of mankind. John must be smiling now, as his cousin continues to poke at satan.

Yet, amidst the anticipation and contemplation, there is also a sense of trepidation. The road that lies ahead is bound to be fraught with challenges and hardships. We must prepare ourselves for what is to come, for the journey that Jesus embarks upon will test his faith, strength, and resolve like never before.

In this pivotal moment, we need to stand by his side, offering unwavering support and love. Let us be a source of solace when doubts arise and a beacon of hope when darkness threatens to overshadow the path. Together, we will navigate the uncertainties, trusting that Jesus' steps are guided by a divine plan.

As I ponder these possibilities, let us not forget the lessons we have learned from Jesus. His compassion, wisdom, and unwavering commitment to his purpose have inspired us all. May we draw strength from his example as we embark on this new chapter of his journey.

Let us keep a watchful eye on the unfolding events, ready to provide comfort, encouragement, and unyielding loyalty. The path that Jesus walks is one that will forever alter the course of history. Let us be witnesses to his divine mission, embracing the magnitude of his calling with reverence and gratitude.

Together, let us stand firm, for the Lamb of God has set foot on a sacred path, and we have the privilege of walking alongside him in this extraordinary chapter of his story.

As we reflect on the profound significance of Jesus being seen on his way to Bethabara, a memory stirs within me—one that echoes the power of sacrificial redemption. It harkens back to the time when our ancestors, the Israelites, were instructed to paint the blood of an unblemished lamb on their door frames on the eve of the Passover.

That sacrificial lamb's blood served as a shield, protecting the innocent from the grips of evil? It was a poignant reminder that through the shedding of blood, salvation was granted to those who believed and followed the divine instructions.

As John hailed Jesus as the "Lamb of God," we discern a profound parallel to that ancient story. The Lamb of God, too, carries the weight of redemption upon his shoulders. His steps echo the sacrificial lamb of old, whose blood was shed to save the innocent.

In Jesus, we find a lamb unblemished and pure, destined to offer himself for the sins of humanity. Just as the Israelites trusted in the blood of the lamb to deliver them from evil, we now place our trust in Jesus, the Lamb of God, to deliver us from the bondage of sin and darkness.

The road to Bethabara, where this declaration was made, becomes a bridge connecting the ancient stories of deliverance and the imminent sacrifice that will bring about a new covenant. The Lamb of God walks in the footsteps of those who have come before him, bearing the hopes and prayers of a world in need of salvation.

With every step he takes toward Bethabara, I imagine the weight of his purpose grows more palpable. He carries within him the hopes and dreams of generations, embracing the destiny foretold since ancient times. Through his sacrifice, a new Passover unfolds—one that will free mankind from the chains of sin and offer eternal life to those who believe.

As I ponder the journey that lies ahead for Jesus, I must remember the significance of the Passover lamb. To acknowledge the power of sacrificial redemption and the profound love that fuels it. The Lamb of God walks a path paved with selflessness, inviting us to partake in the blessings of eternal life.

As we stand alongside Jesus on this sacred journey, may our hearts be adorned with the blood of the unblemished Lamb, symbolizing our faith, trust, and surrender. Let us be a living testament to the transformative power of sacrifice and redemption, drawing strength from the ancient stories and embracing the new chapter unfolding before us.

With each passing day, let us keep the memory of the Passover lamb alive within us, honoring the sacrifice that has paved the way for our own salvation, as well as those who follow behind us. And as we witness Jesus' walking toward his destiny, may our spirits be uplifted, our resolve strengthened, and our gratitude deepened for the Lamb of God who walks among us.

To Pray with Mary and Martha

My dear wife, as I stood there contemplating the significance of Jesus being seen on his way to Bethabara, a sense of urgency filled my heart. It was then that a somber thought crossed my mind—an ominous cloud casting a shadow over our souls. News had reached me that our great friends, Mary and Martha, were grieving the loss of their beloved brother, Lazarus.

Lazarus had fallen ill, succumbing to an illness that had taken hold of him with alarming swiftness. It seemed unfathomable that such a vibrant and cherished soul could be snatched away from us in a matter of days. His sisters, Mary and Martha were pillars of strength, pillars of faith, and pillars of love. Our bond with them ran deep, nurtured by years of shared experiences, laughter, and tears. Our hearts ached for them, knowing the depths of their sorrow and the weight of their loss.

But beyond our concern for our dear friends Mary and Martha, another thought lingered—our hope to see Jesus and his mother, Mary. They were so close to Mary, Martha and Lazarus. Jesus had a particular closeness, an agape love for Lazarus. We yearned for their presence, their comforting embrace in times of grief. In the wake of Lazarus' passing, we felt an urgent calling to be by their side, to console all of them and find solace in their company as well.

Mary, held a special place in our hearts, for I know how much she loved my brother Joseph. We had watched them raise their son with love and tenderness, witnessing the wisdom and grace that emanated from him. Our souls longed to see her, to offer our support and love during this tumultuous time.

Without delay, we made the decision to travel immediately to Bethany, where our friends resided. The journey was arduous for us, physically and emotionally, but our hearts were determined. We carried within us a yearning to be there for Mary and Martha, to share their sorrow and lend them our strength.

As we embarked on the road to Bethany, memories flooded my mind—moments spent in the company of Lazarus, witnessing his laughter, his kindness, and the love that flowed so effortlessly from his soul. He was more than a friend; he was family—a brother of the heart. The thought of his absence created a void within me, one that yearned to be filled by the memories we held so dear.

Our path was paved with uncertainty, yet hope fueled our steps. We believed in the power of miracles, in the transformative touch of Jesus. We knew that even in the darkest of times, a glimmer of light could emerge, igniting hope where there seemed to be none.

As we neared Bethany, anticipation and trepidation intertwined within our beings. Our eyes searched the horizon for any sign of Jesus and his mother, longing for their familiar faces and the solace they brought. The weight of our purpose settled upon us, reminding us of the deep connection we shared with Mary, Martha, and Lazarus.

The village of Bethany came into view, and our hearts beat faster. We knew that within its boundaries lay a family in mourning, a family in need of our presence and support. With each passing step, the reality of Lazarus' absence grew more profound, the realization of our mission pressing upon us like a stone upon our hearts.

The thoughts raced in our minds as we searched the depths of our own faith to strengthen theirs. We knew we needed to draw strength to show our love for Mary and Martha, an mourn the loss of Lazarus with them. We will have to carry their burdens as our own, offering solace, compassion, and unwavering support. Our journey to Bethany is not merely a physical one; it is a pilgrimage of the heart—a testament to the bond we share and the love that binds us all.

I suggested to Mary that as we will enter the realm of grief and loss, may our presence bring comfort, our words offer solace, and our love provide a balm for their wounded souls. And within the embrace of our dear friends, I pray we, too, find healing and renewal, as we navigate the profound mysteries of life and death, knowing that in our unity lies the strength to endure.

Together, my dear Mary, let us walk this path of compassion, guided by the flickering light of hope, and upheld by the everlasting bonds of love.

The sun began its descent, casting a warm golden glow over the village of Bethany as we approached the home of Mary, Martha, and Lazarus. The air was heavy with grief, and the somber atmosphere enveloped us as we entered their abode.

Upon our arrival, we were met with tear-stained faces and embraces that spoke volumes—wordless expressions of pain, loss, and the deep well of love that bound us together. The sorrow in their eyes mirrored our own, and in that shared understanding, we found solace.

As Mary recognized they hadn't eaten, she took to the kitchen to prepare something to eat with the food we brought. Mary, Martha, and I sat together, the weight of our collective grief hanging heavy in the air. The memory of Lazarus lingered in every corner of their home—the echo of his laughter, the warmth of his presence, and the void that his absence had left behind. The room was filled with memories, both joyous and heartrending, intermingling to form a tapestry of love and loss.

In the midst of our collective sorrow, whispers began to circulate—a rumor carried on the winds of hope and desperation. It was said that Jesus, the one we had sought in our time of need, was approaching Bethany. The mere mention of his name infused the room with a surge of anticipation and renewed faith.

Mary, the mother of Jesus, entered the room, her eyes filled with a mixture of pain and resilience. She was a beacon of strength, emanating a quiet power that commanded respect and reverence. In her presence, we felt the love of a mother who had borne the weight of the world on her shoulders—a mother who had witnessed her son's miracles and understood the depth of his divine purpose.

Mary said that Jesus stopped about 100 yards from the house and told her to go ahead, he would be there soon. She said she looked back at Him, and He was leaning against a fencepost looking at the hill where he knew the body of Lazarus was placed. As Mary shared the news of Jesus' impending arrival, a flicker of hope ignited within all of our hearts. We clung to the belief that his presence could bring about a miraculous turn of events, that the sting of death could be transformed into a celebration of life. In our darkest hour, we yearned for the touch of the one who had the power to heal, to resurrect, and to bring forth the light.

The air crackled with expectation, as if the very essence of life was hanging in the balance. We understood that Jesus had the ability to defy the laws of nature, to breathe life into the lifeless, and to restore hope where it had been extinguished.

And then, as if in response to our collective prayers, Jesus appeared on the threshold of the house. His eyes, filled with compassion and understanding, met ours, and a wave of comfort washed over us. In that moment, we knew that we were not alone, that our grief and pain were shared burdens that he carried in his heart.

Mary and Martha, overcome with emotions, fell at Jesus' feet, their tears mingling with words of longing and anguish. In the depths of their sorrow, they poured out their hearts, recounting their love for Lazarus and the pain of his loss. Jesus listened, his presence a balm for their wounded spirits, his words carrying the weight of divine reassurance.

Jesus, filled with emotion and pity, said He wanted to see Lazarus. He said, "Have the men come and roll the stone away". Martha reminded Him that Lazarus had been dead for four days, that there would be an odor. His mom turned to Martha and said "Do as He tells you". So she called for the men of the village to roll away the stone.

I watched, my heart swelling with gratitude and awe, as Jesus approached the tomb where Lazarus had been laid to rest. The atmosphere grew hushed, as if the very universe held its breath, awaiting the unfolding of a miracle. In that sacred moment, I witnessed the power of Jesus' love—a love that transcended the boundaries of life and death, offering a glimmer of hope in the face of seemingly insurmountable loss.

With a voice that resonated with authority and tenderness, Jesus commanded, "Lazarus, come out!" And in a moment that defied all logic and understanding, Lazarus emerged from the tomb—a living testament to the power of faith, love, and the eternal spirit that dwells within us all.

Joy erupted from the depths of our souls as we witnessed the miraculous reunion of Lazarus and his grieving sisters. The room was filled with laughter, tears of joy, and a profound sense of awe. In that moment, we knew that our journey to Bethany had not been in vain—that our presence, our love, and our unwavering faith had played a part in the unfolding of a divine masterpiece.

As we embraced one another, our hearts overflowing with gratitude, I realized that this was a moment of profound transformation—for Lazarus, for Mary and Martha, and for all of us who had been touched by the hand of Jesus. The resurrection of Lazarus signified not only the power of Jesus to conquer death but also the promise of new life and the eternal hope that rests in the embrace of divine love.

Now, as I recount these events, I am filled with a sense of awe and reverence. Our journey to Bethany was not merely a physical one—it was a pilgrimage of the spirit, a testament to the unbreakable bonds of love and faith that unite us all. In the face of grief, we discovered the transformative power of Jesus' love—a love that conquers death, transcends human understanding, and offers us the promise of eternal life.

May the memory of Lazarus' resurrection forever remain etched in our hearts, a reminder that even in the depths of despair, miracles can unfold, and hope can be resurrected. Let us carry this profound truth with us as we continue our journey, knowing that the love and power of Jesus will guide us through the darkest nights, lighting our path with unwavering grace and mercy.

Back to Jerusalem by way of Jericho

As the sun rose over the village of Bethany, my wife Mary and I prepared for a momentous journey. The news had spread like wildfire that Jesus, the miraculous healer and teacher, would be making his way to Jerusalem. This was an opportunity we could not miss. Alongside Jesus would be his mother Mary, his faithful disciples, and a growing crowd of followers. We eagerly joined them, our hearts filled with anticipation.

The distance from Bethany to Jerusalem was only about two miles, a short walk for most. But Jesus, always filled with purpose and determination, set off in a different direction. He led us toward Jericho, and without hesitation, we followed. The path was rugged and winding, the dusty road seeming to stretch endlessly before us.

As we descended Jerusalem Hill from Bethany, Jesus halted, his eyes filled with a mixture of sadness and resolve. Sensing the weight of his words, he gathered his disciples close, and we huddled around him, eager to hear his message. With a voice that carried both strength and vulnerability, Jesus spoke of the days to come.

"For the third and final time," he began, "I must tell you that the evil one will conspire with many people to turn against me. They will crucify me when we reach Jerusalem. But fear not, for after three days, I will triumph over death and rise again."

The weight of his words hung heavy in the air, and silence enveloped us. We had known of the impending crucifixion, but to hear it from Jesus himself made it all too real. We exchanged glances filled with concern and sorrow, yet hope flickered within our hearts. Jesus had promised victory over death, and we clung to that promise.

As we continued our journey towards Jericho, the news of Jesus' impending crucifixion spread among the group. Whispers and murmurs filled the air, and a sense of heaviness settled upon us all. It was during this solemn time that James and John's mother, known to us as Zebadee's wife, found an opportunity to approach Jesus.

With humility and love in her eyes, she knelt before him, her voice trembling slightly as she spoke, "Lord, when you come into your kingdom, would you grant that my sons may sit at your right and left hand?"

Jesus turned his gaze towards her, his expression gentle yet tinged with sadness. He understood her desire, but he knew what lay ahead for him. With a tender smile, he replied, "You do not know what you are asking? Can they drink the cup that I am about to drink?"

Confusion clouded her face, but she nodded, her faith unshaken. "Yes, Lord," she answered, "they will drink from your cup, for they are your devoted followers."

Jesus' gaze shifted to James and John; his voice filled with reassurance. "Indeed, you shall drink from my cup," he said, "but the places at my right and left hand are not mine to grant. They belong to those for whom they have been prepared by my Father."

In that moment, a deeper understanding dawned upon us. Jesus had made it clear that his journey would end in crucifixion, but he also hinted at the ultimate triumph that would follow. We marveled at his unwavering commitment, knowing that the path he walked would not be easy, yet trusting in his divine purpose.

With a heavy heart and a renewed sense of determination, we pressed on towards Jericho. The road stretched out before us, but we walked with a newfound resolve, ready to face whatever lay ahead. Jesus had spoken of his impending death, but he had also assured us of his victory over death itself. We clung to his words, our hope burning bright, as we continued our journey towards Jerusalem, the city that held both pain and promise.

Help Them See, Walk and Preach Love

It was a journey filled with anticipation and excitement as my wife Mary and I continued on toward Jericho, about 7 miles away alongside Jesus, His mother Mary, and the dedicated disciples. The dusty roads stretched before us, as if leading us toward a destiny we were yet to fully comprehend.

Jericho awaited us, a city abuzz with whispers of the Messiah's arrival. The news had spread at lightning speed, and a throng of people awaited Jesus, yearning for a glimpse of His divine presence. We made our way through the bustling streets, the air electric with anticipation.

As we entered the city, I couldn't help but feel the weight of responsibility on my shoulders. We were witnesses to miracles, bearers of a message that could transform lives. Jesus had been teaching us the ways of agape love, a love that transcended all boundaries and offered healing to those who were blind to the truth.

It wasn't long before the need for such healing presented itself. We encountered Bartimaeus, a blind beggar whose desperate cries echoed through the streets. His sightless eyes held a glimmer of hope as he begged for mercy and assistance.

My heart ached for Bartimaeus, for I knew what it was like to be blind to the truth. I had experienced the transformative power of Jesus' love firsthand, and I believed that Bartimaeus too deserved to see the world in all its glory.

Approaching Jesus, I shared Bartimaeus' story, urging our Teacher to show him the same compassion and love He had bestowed upon us. Jesus listened intently, His gaze filled with understanding and empathy.

He turned His attention to Bartimaeus, and with a voice that commanded attention, called the blind man forward.

The crowd parted as Bartimaeus made his way toward Jesus, his steps guided by a mixture of hope and uncertainty. I watched with bated breath as Jesus reached out His hand and gently touched Bartimaeus' eyes. The air crackled with a lightning like energy as the blind man's world was transformed.

Bartimaeus' eyes fluttered open, and a look of wonder and amazement washed over his face. The darkness that had shrouded his vision was replaced with vibrant colors and newfound clarity. Tears streamed down his cheeks as he beheld the world around him for the first time.

A chorus of joyful exclamations erupted from the onlookers, their voices blending in a symphony of awe and gratitude. The entire town knew Bartimaeus had been blind from an injury when he was 5 years old and now, he had been given the gift of sight, a physical manifestation of the deeper truth that Jesus had come to reveal.

In that moment, I understood the lesson Jesus sought to teach us all. There were those among us who were blind, not merely in their physical sight but in their understanding of the love and grace that encompassed us. Jesus' healing of Bartimaeus served as a powerful reminder to be patient with those who were blind to the truth, for they had never experienced the transformative power of agape love.

As the city of Jericho continued to buzz with anticipation, Jesus turned His attention to Zacchaeus, a man whose blindness was of a different nature. Zacchaeus, a tax collector despised by many, had climbed a sycamore tree in an attempt to catch a glimpse of Jesus. Little did he know that God's plan had been set in motion long before he even reached for the first branch.

Jesus' eyes met Zacchaeus' gaze, a knowing smile gracing His lips. He called the tax collector down from the tree, inviting Himself to Zacchaeus' home that evening. In that act, Jesus revealed that the

Father had planted a seed, a tree, that would provide Zacchaeus with the vantage point he needed to see beyond the crowd. The Father's Plan was not a play-by-play plan, it was well thought out from the beginning of time to the end of time. The only thing missing was how we each react to our free will then he changed and changed the plan until we were safe or we were set in our ways to stray from eternal life with Him.

Zacchaeus' heart swelled with a mix of disbelief and gratitude as he welcomed Jesus into his home. In the presence of the Messiah, he began to comprehend the plan that God had for each of us, a plan that involved redemption, forgiveness, and a love that embraced even the most lost among us.

As the sun began to set over the city of Jericho, I pondered the lessons I had learned that day. Jesus had shown us that true sight went beyond the physical, that it encompassed an understanding of God's love and the purpose He had for each of our lives. I knew that the journey with Jesus was far from over, and that there were more miracles, more lessons, and more lives to be transformed.

It was a beautiful evening, the multitude of stars shining brightly as we sat around the campfire at Zacchaeus' house, we chatted about what had happened and what we learned.

Simon Peter was the first to speak, saying "With each healing touch and compassionate word, Jesus brings hope and restoration to those who had been broken by life's hardships. The blind receives their sight, the lame walk, and the hearts of the lost were filled with newfound purpose. It is as if the very fabric of Jericho was being rewoven with threads of redemption."

His brother Andrew spoke up "Amidst the outward miracles, Jesus recognizes the blindness that resides within the hearts of many. There are those who were blind to their own brokenness, their need for forgiveness and healing. We all need to be aware of that! They live their lives in pursuit of worldly riches and power, blinded to the eternal treasures that awaits them."

Philip said, "We walked through the streets of Jericho, Jesus paused beneath a majestic Sycamore tree. His gaze fixed upon its branches, and a familiar smile crossed His face. He turned to me and whispered, 'Philip, do you see this tree? It holds a story of divine providence.'" My curiosity piqued and I listened as Jesus unfolded a tale of God's intricate plan. He revealed that long before Zacchaeus ever climbed that tree, the Father had planted a seed—a seed that would grow into the very tree with the very branch Zacchaeus would reach for Him to see You, Jesus"

The realization of God's foresight left me in awe. Jesus beckoned to Zacchaeus, who was standing in the midst of the crowd, drawn by an invisible force to the presence of the Messiah. As Zacchaeus approached, a mixture of anticipation and trepidation painted his features.

When Jesus smiled warmly at him, saying, "Zacchaeus, come down immediately. I must stay at your house today", the crowd murmured in disbelief, for Zacchaeus was a tax collector, known for his greed and dishonesty.

Zacchaeus threw another log on the fire and said "At that moment, experienced a profound revelation. The love and acceptance extended to me by Jesus shattered the barriers I had built around his heart. I recognized the blindness that had clouded my judgment and all the selfish pursuits that had consumed my life."

Jesus' eyes sparkled with joy and satisfaction as He responded, "Today salvation has come to this house because this man, also is a son of Abraham. For the Son of Man came to seek and to save the lost. I was moved with the transformation in Zacchaeus! It was so profound! His encounter with Jesus had opened his eyes to the truth that had eluded him for so long. The seed of redemption had taken root within his heart, and its branches stretched out, touching every aspect of his life."

Thomas said "As I reflect on the lessons Jesus had imparted to us, I recall through the healing of Bartimaeus and calling Zacchaeus, Jesus had shown us the need for patience and compassion. Some were blind to the truth, while others were blind to their own brokenness. Yet, in His infinite wisdom, Jesus saw beyond their shortcomings and extended His love to all."

As the embers of our campfire glow began to dance their last, I thought about how our journey with Jesus was far from over, but in Jericho, we had witnessed the power of agape love in an entirely different level. It had the ability to heal the blind, both physically and spiritually. It had the power to transform hearts and unveil the plan God had for each of us.

As we prepared to leave Jericho the next day, I carried with me a renewed sense of purpose. I would strive to extend the same love and compassion that Jesus had shown, knowing that within every person, there existed a seed of redemption waiting to bloom.

Back to Bethany?

The sun beat down upon us as we set out on yet another journey with Jesus, His mother Mary, and the disciples. Our destination - the village of Bethany – again! Excitement coursed through our veins as we anticipated the events that would unfold during our time there. But why did the Master want to go back to Bethany?

Bethany held a special place in our hearts, for it was the home of our dear friends Mary, Martha, and Lazarus. It was in Bethany that Lazarus had experienced a miracle—the raising of the dead. Jesus' power and love had brought him back from the clutches of the grave, and we were filled with gratitude.

As we approached Bethany, a sense of celebration filled the air. The villagers had heard of Lazarus' resurrection and were eager to express their joy and gratitude. Mary, Martha, and Lazarus had planned a thanksgiving feast at the home of Simon the Leper, a man who had also experienced Jesus' transformative touch.

The streets of Bethany were adorned with flowers and decorations, a vibrant display of the village's exuberance. The sound of laughter and music mingled with the delicious aroma of cooking, signaling the festivities that awaited us.

When we arrived at Simon's home, we were greeted with warm embraces and heartfelt gratitude. The room buzzed with excitement as people shared stories of Lazarus' miraculous return to life. The atmosphere was a testament to the power and love of Jesus.

As the feast began, Lazarus sat at the center of the table, a living testimony to Jesus' power over death. His face, once marked by the pastiness of the grave, now radiated with life. Yet, amidst the jubilant celebration, there was a sense of solemnity that clung to Lazarus.

I watched him closely, trying to discern the source of his quiet contemplation. And then, it became clear—Lazarus was unable to smile. The resurrection had brought him back from the brink of eternal rest, but it had left an indelible mark upon him. His physical body had been restored, but his smile had been lost forever.

In that moment, I realized the profound lesson that Lazarus' lost smile held for us all. It was a reminder that life, even in its most miraculous form, was fleeting. Lazarus had been so close to the eternal life that awaited him in heaven, and yet, he had been called back to this earthly existence.

His inability to smile would forever serve as a testimony to the transient nature of our earthly existence. It was a reminder to cherish each moment, to live fully and embrace the opportunities presented to us. Lazarus' smile, forever lost, was a symbol of the ultimate surrender to God's plan, even in the face of death, as we know the glorious life that awaits us on the other side!

Amidst the solemn celebration, another profound moment unfolded. Mary, the sister of Martha and Lazarus, approached Jesus with a jar of expensive perfume. Her eyes glimmered with a mixture of adoration and reverence as she knelt before Him.

With a tender gesture, Mary poured the fragrant perfume onto Jesus' feet and began to wipe them with her hair. The room fell into a hushed silence as the powerful act of love unfolded before our eyes. With the sweet smell of this perfume permeating the entire room, it was a moment of profound devotion, an expression of deep gratitude and love for the Savior.

Mary's act of anointing Jesus' feet with perfume held a reflective significance. In that act, she recognized the true value of God Himself, present before her in the form of Jesus. Her response was one of loving worship, a pouring out of her heart's deepest affections. I thought, that through her actions, we find inspiration for our own relationships with God. Her act of devotion challenges us to fully receive and give love, to recognize the immense value of God in our lives. It reminds us to approach Him with reverence, gratitude, and a willingness to pour out our hearts in worship.

Mary's act of love reverberated in our hearts, reminding us of the transformative power of love itself. It was a love that transcended boundaries, that moved hearts, and that compelled us to respond with our own acts of devotion.

In that moment, I realized that love was not merely a sentiment or an emotion—it was an action. It had the power to move us, to transform us, and to draw us closer to the heart of God. Mary's act of anointing was a tangible expression of that truth, an invitation for each of us to love God with all that we are.

As the feast continued, we savored the food, the laughter, and the stories shared. But the memory of Lazarus' lost smile and Mary's act of devotion remained etched in our hearts. They were reminders of the brevity of life and the depth of love, urging us to live fully and embrace the opportunities to love and worship our Creator.

Plan for Tomorrow

After the neighbors left, Jesus asked Mary and I to gather the disciples to the far corner of the room so He could explain the plan for tomorrow. After they congregated and settled down, Jesus stood up and said that He wanted everyone to be on board with His plan for tomorrow. He said, "I want you to know that I am the Alpha and the Omega."

He continued, "As you all know, we have been fighting the war between good and evil. I love all the Chief Priests, Pharisees, Elders and Scribes. I love them all! Heck, I created them all! They are good people but sometimes good people can't seem to tie their own sandal straps! They think about everything in terms of how they will benefit instead of what is best for everyone. They tend to love themselves much more than their own families."

He said, "But I want to give them all the benefit of last chances. We gave all of you the gift of free will to choose the right path or the wrong path. We do everything we can to help each one of you to make good decisions. I am more than willing to do this for them. My fight is not with them, it is with lucifer and the third of my angels he took with him. The only way he thinks he can win is to trick good people to make bad choices and then leave them in the fiery darkness of Gahanna."

"Tomorrow, I am going to fulfill the prophecy found in the Old Testament in the book of Zechariah. Zechariah 9:9 states, 'Rejoice greatly, Daughter Zion! Shout, Daughter Jerusalem! See, your king comes to you, righteous and victorious, lowly and riding on a donkey, on a colt, the foal of a donkey.'"

By riding a donkey into Jerusalem, I will intentionally fulfill this prophecy to symbolize that I am the long-awaited Messiah, the King of Israel. The act of riding a donkey, a humble and peaceful animal, will signify my humility and the peaceful nature of his kingdom.

Jesus continued "I want the Chief Priests and Sanhedrin to be able to recognize me as not only your king, but theirs as well. I want to demonstrate that they should not feel threatened by me, but they should worry about the consequences of their actions if they choose to try to implement the evil deeds of satan."

He concluded with "but make no mistake, My Plan is THE PLAN that eventually will win! I will allow some to work with satan to persecute and put me to death on a tree. By that action, I conquer sin for those to choose good over evil. I know there are many who will choose good, and I have reserved a place for them in My Father's House. Satan never will get them and he will be left with himself and his loser demons, the original one third who I gave them the choice to leave with him"

Let's get to sleep so we can get on with the plan in the morning!

Witnessing the Arrival of the Prince of Peace

I stood alongside my wife Mary, anticipation and excitement filling the air as we stood inside the Eastern gate of Jerusalem. The sun beamed down, casting a golden glow on the city, and the buzz of anticipation was palpable as people lined the streets, awaiting the arrival of Jesus, the humble King riding on a donkey. My heart beat faster, for they all had heard tales of Jesus' miracles, his wisdom, and his message of hope and peace. Today, on this auspicious day, I hoped to catch a glimpse of the man who had captivated the hearts of so many.

As the crowd grew thicker, I could feel a surge of energy emanating from the people around him. The sound of excited chatter filled his ears, a symphony of anticipation that seemed to grow louder with each passing moment. The scent of dust and warm earth hung in the air, mingling with the aroma of freshly cut palm fronds that had been strewn across the path in honor of the approaching Messiah.

I looked around, taking in the vibrant scene. The streets were lined with men, women, and children, all eagerly awaiting the arrival of Jesus. Some wore their finest garments, their robes shimmering in the sunlight, while others, like Mary and me, wore more humble attire, our faces etched with reverence and hope.

As the distant murmur of the crowd began to increase, I strained my eyes to catch a glimpse of the approaching procession. I saw a wave of movement rippling through the multitude of people, as if an invisible current was passing through them. People began to raise their voices in jubilant praise, shouting "Hosanna!" and waving their palm branches in the air.

And then he saw him.

Jesus, riding atop a humble donkey, approached with a calm and regal presence. His dark hair fell gently upon his shoulders, and his eyes, filled with compassion and love, seemed to connect with each person he passed. I felt a surge of warmth envelop my being, as if I was standing in the presence of something truly divine.

The sound of the crowd intensified, echoing through the streets like thunder. The clatter of hooves against the cobblestones mixed with the cheers and cries of the people. Mary and I joined in, our voices rising in praise and adoration. The air seemed to vibrate with the energy of the moment, and we could hardly contain our joy.

As Jesus drew nearer, I panned the crowd to catch some glimpses of the expressions on people's faces. There were tears of gratitude streaming down the cheeks of some, while others wore looks of awe and wonderment. The children, their eyes wide with excitement, ran alongside the procession, their laughter blending with the joyful noise of the crowd.

Amidst the discordance of sounds, I noticed the soft melody of a lyre being played by a street musician. The gentle strumming added a melodic layer to the jubilant atmosphere, enhancing the sense of reverence and celebration that permeated the air. The music seemed to dance in harmony with the collective heartbeat of the crowd.

The smell of crushed palm fronds and the distant aroma of spices wafted through the air, creating a heady mix of scents. I could also catch whiffs of freshly baked bread and roasted lamb, as families prepared their Passover feasts. The mingling aromas enveloped us, reminding us of the rich traditions and the significance of this holy season.

As Jesus rode past Mary and I, our eyes locked on Him for a fleeting moment. In that brief connection, I felt a surge of love and understanding pass between us. I sensed that Jesus saw into the depths of my soul, recognizing my hopes, fears, and aspirations. It was as if time stood still, and in that moment, we knew that our lives had been forever changed.

The procession moved on, disappearing into the distance, but the spirit of that day lingered within us. We felt a renewed sense of hope, a flame of faith that burned brighter within their hearts. We knew that we had been witness to something extraordinary, something that would shape the course of history.

Mary and I stood there for a while longer, taking in the atmosphere of the city and reflecting on the significance of the day. We knew that the arrival of Jesus as the Prince of Peace marked the beginning of a new era, one filled with love, compassion, and the promise of salvation.

As we turned to make our way back to Bethany, we felt a renewed sense of purpose. We vowed to follow Jesus, to spread his message of love and peace, and to share the story of that momentous day when the humble King entered Jerusalem on a donkey, heralded by the adoration of the people.

And so, we walked away from the Eastern gate, our hearts filled with gratitude and a sense of divine presence. We carried with us the sights, sounds, and smells of that special occasion, etching them into their memories, forever changed by the encounter with Jesus, the Prince of Peace.

Love's Battle: Confronting Corruption and Embracing Redemption

I woke with a startle as a gentle hand shook my shoulder. Blinking the sleep from my eyes, I focused on the face of Jesus, his eyes filled with determination and purpose. It was still early morning in Bethany, and the sun had just begun to cast its soft glow over the sleepy town.

"Cleopas," he said softly, his voice carrying an air of urgency, "we must make our way to the Temple in Jerusalem."

His words struck me like lightning, jolting me awake. I quickly roused my companions, Peter and James, who were sharing the same humble dwelling with me. Within moments, we were on our feet, ready to embark on the journey Jesus had set before us.

As the sun began to rise over the eastern hills of Bethany, it served to light the way up the hill to Jerusalem. I felt a mixture of excitement and trepidation. Today was a crucial day, one that would test the very fabric of our faith. Jesus was my brother Joseph's son, whom he nurtured the Blessed Mother Mary through her pregnancy, traveled to Egypt to save them from the tyrant Harrod, then fed Him physically, emotionally and Spiritually in Nazareth until he died. This is the least I could do for me wonderful nephew.

As we walked together, the crisp morning air filled my lungs, invigorating me with a sense of anticipation. The road stretched out before us, winding through the countryside, gradually leading us closer to the heart of Jerusalem. The scent of earth and dew clung to the air, mingling with the sweet fragrance of blooming flowers and the distant aroma of breakfast fires.

As we made our way, Jesus seemed lost in thought, his gaze fixed on the surroundings. Suddenly, he veered off the path towards a fig tree, its branches void of fruit. With disappointment etched on his face, Jesus uttered words that struck a chord within me, words laden with symbolism and meaning.

"May no one ever eat fruit from you again," he said to the fig tree, his voice tinged with sorrow.

I could sense the confusion in Peter and James' eyes, and I, too, sought to understand the lesson behind Jesus' actions. He turned to us, his expression filled with solemnity, and explained the significance of the fig tree. It was a representation of fruitlessness, a reminder that when the time for bearing fruit arrives, one should not be found lacking.

We walked in silence, the rhythmic sound of our footsteps on the dusty road providing a steady cadence to our thoughts. Jesus seemed deep in contemplation, his gaze fixed on the path ahead, as if he was already immersed in the divine plan unfolding before us.

The road was teeming with people, fellow pilgrims and locals making their way to the temple. The air was filled with the scent of freshly baked bread and the earthy aroma of livestock. The buzz of conversations and the occasional laughter filled the air, but I couldn't help but notice an undercurrent of tension, like a storm brewing on the horizon.

The journey continued, and our steps quickened as we approached the bustling streets of Jerusalem. The city thrummed with activity, the sounds of vendors hawking their wares, the clip-clop of donkeys' hooves on cobblestones, and the buzz of conversations enveloping us. The atmosphere crackled with anticipation, for it was the week of Passover, and pilgrims from all corners of the land had flocked to Jerusalem.

As we neared the temple, the atmosphere grew denser. The ornate architecture of the temple walls loomed before us, its grandeur contrasting with the heaviness in my heart. I could see the chief priests, scribes, and elders, adorned in their elaborate robes, gathered near the entrance. Their stern faces and calculating eyes betrayed their true motives.

Jesus approached them, his gentle demeanor radiating a love that transcended their hardened hearts. He spoke with wisdom and authority, his words cutting through the layers of self-interest and corruption. I listened intently as he offered them a chance to see the truth, to witness the love of God incarnate standing right before them.

Their responses were laced with skepticism and thinly veiled animosity. They questioned his authority, challenging him at every turn. Their words dripped with venom, betraying the darkness that had consumed their souls long ago. Yet, Jesus remained steadfast, offering them grace even in the face of their unyielding resistance.

He exposed their hypocrisy, their misguided pursuits of power and control. His words struck at the core of their being, shaking the foundations of their false piety. But despite their hardened hearts, Jesus never wavered in his love for them. He desired their redemption, their transformation, and he was willing to pay the ultimate price to make it possible.

Peter, James and I scanned the temple to see if this dialog Jesus was having was creating a stir within the rest of those moving about. Most were just carrying on their objectives of the morning, unaware of the tension building within the chief priests and scribes. The outer court teemed with merchants and money changers, their stalls and tables filled with animals for sacrifice, and the clinking of coins reverberated in the air.

Jesus, his eyes filled with righteous anger, took a seat and gestured for us to join him. As we settled down, he quietly observed the goings-on around us, his gaze sweeping across the scene. Gradually, his eyes narrowed, and a storm brewed within his heart. The once hallowed ground, His Father's house, had become a marketplace, a den of commercialization.

With purposeful determination, Jesus rose to his feet, his cloak billowing around him. In that moment, I saw a side of him I had not witnessed before – a righteous zeal that burned like fire. His hands reached out, deftly weaving cords into a whip.

In the consecrated temple, the air hung heavy with the scent of incense and the weight of expectation. Jesus, usually calm and compassionate, felt an intensity welling up within him that could no longer be contained. His eyes rapidly moving left and right across the bustling courtyard, where merchants and money changers preyed upon the devout seeking redemption. He saw the desperation in their eyes, their faith burdened by the yoke of tradition and the insidious grip of greed.

With a voice that commanded attention, Jesus vented his frustrations to those gathered, condemning their actions in no uncertain terms. He spoke of his Father's house, a place intended for worship and reverence, now desecrated by greed and exploitation. His words thundered through the air, piercing the hearts of those who heard.

With a righteous fury burning in his heart, Jesus made his way through the chaos. The cages that held innocent sacrificial animals captive, their eyes filled with fear and longing for freedom, became his first target. The Son of God, who came to offer himself as the ultimate sacrifice, saw the injustice of those who sought to profit from the redemption of others. His voice boomed through the temple, his words piercing through the noise and echoing against the sacred walls.

And then, He spoke of a coming sacrifice, a sacrifice that would render the need for animal offerings obsolete. He spoke of himself, his impending crucifixion, and the atonement of sins that would follow. A sense of awe settled over us, a realization that we stood in the presence of the Lamb of God, who would offer himself for the redemption of humanity.

"The only sacrifice," he declared, his voice reverberating with authority, "will be me, the Son of God, to take away the sins of the world." With a single gesture, the cages flew open, releasing the animals from their bonds. The startled creatures scampered away, liberated from the clutches of a system that had lost sight of its true purpose.

Jesus then turned his gaze to the money changers, their tables adorned with coins and weighted with the love of wealth. The flicker of anger in his eyes reflected the divine disappointment. "Love of money," he proclaimed, "is the root of all evil." With swift and deliberate movements, he overturned the tables, sending coins scattering and chaos reigning. The symbols of materialism, the very embodiment of misplaced priorities, were reduced to a disarray of shattered illusions.

For Jesus, it was not the ritualistic buying of sacrificial animals that pleased the Father, the Spirit, or Himself. It was the profound transformation of hearts, the genuine repentance that stemmed from a deep understanding of divine love. His actions in the temple were a powerful testament to his unwavering commitment to unveiling the truth, to showing humanity a better way.

In that moment of righteous indignation, Jesus embodied the profound love of the Father, the Spirit, and the Son. His frustration and anger at the perversion of sacred rites were driven by an unwavering desire to guide humanity toward a genuine, transformative relationship with God. The temple, once a symbol of divine worship, had been corrupted by the very hands meant to uphold its sanctity. Jesus, in his unparalleled righteousness, sought to restore its true essence, challenging the status quo and pointing to a path rooted in love, compassion, and selflessness.

The air was charged with anticipation and conviction. The sights and sounds of the Temple faded into the background as his words filled our ears and hearts. We were witness to a divine moment, a revelation of the true purpose of the Temple and the coming fulfillment of the Law.

The day wore on, and as we made our way back through the streets of Jerusalem, a hum of excitement and expectancy filled the air. Rumors of Jesus' arrival had spread like wildfire, and anticipation for the events of the coming days grew stronger with each passing moment.

The city buzzed with preparations for Passover, the scent of roasted lamb and freshly baked bread wafting from open doorways. The streets were adorned with colorful banners and garlands, and the sound of children's laughter filled the air as they prepared for the celebration ahead.

As we reached the Eastern gate, where Mary and I had stood just a day prior, the scene unfolded before us once more. The streets were lined with people, their voices rising in joyful praise. Palm branches rustled in the wind, their vibrant green leaves swaying in unison, a symbol of hope and triumph.

The people we saw near the gate knew bits and pieces of what had transpired there. Most had either seen or heard of Jesus's triumphant entrance into Jerusalem, some had been at or near the temple and only absorbed the sights of Jesus showing signs that He was about to take things over. Little did they know that was just part of God's plan to entice the evil one to step things up a notch.

Mary had come to meet us at the gate from Bethany with the others. Now reunited, we joined in the chorus of Hosannas, their hearts brimming with awe and gratitude. They had borne witness to or heard of, Jesus' righteous anger in the Temple, to his proclamation of a new way, and now, they stood ready to embrace the unfolding story of redemption in this bustling city. We were treated with the mingling scents of Passover preparations, and the resounding echoes of praise and adoration. It was a day that would forever be etched in our memories, a prelude to the remarkable events that lay ahead.

As the day wore on, we made our way back down from the temple, retracing our steps towards Bethany. The setting sun cast long shadows on the path, mirroring the heaviness in our hearts. Jesus spoke to us, sharing his divine plan for the Passover meal in the upper room. His voice was gentle, but there was an undeniable determination in his words.

We listened attentively, the gravity of the situation sinking deep within us. We knew that the time was drawing near, that the forces of darkness were closing in. Jesus spoke of love, of sacrifice, and of redemption. His words echoed in our souls, bringing a glimmer of hope amidst the gathering darkness.

As we reached the outskirts of Bethany, the moon bathed the landscape in a soft, ethereal glow. We entered the familiar house where we would prepare for the Passover, our hearts heavy with the weight of what lay ahead. Yet, a sense of purpose and divine assurance permeated the air, reminding us that although the road was treacherous, we were not alone.

In that moment, I realized that Jesus' mission went far beyond the confrontation with the religious leaders. It was a battle against the very forces that had corrupted their hearts, a battle fought with love, truth, and self-sacrifice. And as we gathered around the campfire and ate a simple meal, we talked about what we were about to witness - the culmination of that divine plan—the ultimate act of love that would change the course of history forever.

We knew that in the following days, we would witness the arrest, trial, and crucifixion of our beloved teacher. But amidst the darkness and despair, we held onto the flickering flame of hope. For we knew that Jesus' sacrifice was not in vain, that it was through his death and resurrection that salvation would be offered to all. Jesus told us that this was the Father's Plan and not try to stop it, as it was all part of what would be Salvation History. That Jesus' sole purpose for coming here was to defeat sin and the darkness of sin in our lives, the lives of all who fell asleep before us and those to come.

His war was with the evil one and his minions. His ways deceive the weak, draw them into sin and to pull other innocents with them. A Good Shepherd leaves His flock in search of the lost sheep. That is exactly His Plan and we all vowed to not interrupt that plan, as painful as it was to us emotionally.

And so, as we prepared for the Passover meal, we embraced our roles in this unfolding drama, knowing that through the pain and suffering, a new dawn was about to break—a dawn that would bring redemption, forgiveness, and eternal love to all who would believe.

Love, Betrayal, and Sacrifice

I witnessed Jesus moving from disciple to disciple, washing their feet with a tenderness that pierced my heart, I couldn't help but feel a surge of love and admiration for my nephew. The sight of their dirty, callused feet didn't deter Jesus; instead, he embraced their messiness with open arms. Pouring water over their feet and drying them with a towel, I could sense the love and humility radiating from Jesus.

When Peter protested, refusing to let Jesus wash his feet, I noticed Jesus gently reminding him of the importance of serving others. It was a powerful message that resonated with all of us, especially the men in the room. I understood that this act of service was a call to love and care for everyone, regardless of their circumstances—whether they were dirty, homeless, imprisoned, ill, lame, poor, or rich. Jesus wanted his disciples, including me, to grasp that God's love extended to all, and that love would be displayed in the coming 24 hours.

As I observed the ceremonial aspects of the Passover meal unfolding, I saw the first cup, the Cup of Sanctification, being mixed with water and wine. I watched as the Jesus offered a formal blessing over the cup. The tantalizing aroma of the roasted lamb filled my senses, and the warm glow of the flickering candles illuminated the faces of those gathered around the table. The voices of the disciples intermingled in prayer and song, and the clinking of cups and plates resonated as they passed them from hand to hand.

With a heavy heart, I attentively listened to Jesus' words, his voice piercing my soul. I knew Jesus was referring to Judas, the enigmatic disciple simmering with anger and resentment. I observed the tense atmosphere between Jesus and Judas, noticing how Judas avoided meeting Jesus' gaze. Deep down, I understood that Judas would be the one to betray his beloved nephew. Unfortunately, I knew that someone had to be the one that satan would use to result in Jesus' death.

As Jesus revealed that one of them would betray him, I felt anxiety grip my heart. My mind raced, trying to comprehend the unfolding events. It was unfathomable to believe that one of our own would commit such an act. Yet, I couldn't ignore the guilt and shame etched on Judas' face as he shifted uncomfortably. When Jesus instructed Judas to go and do what he had to, my heart sank, and the mood in the room shifted. I watched in horror as Judas rose from the table and left, his face consumed by fear and anxiety. It marked the beginning of the end.

As the third cup, the Cup of Blessing, was mixed, I strained to catch every word spoken. The supper officially commenced, and we all partook in the lamb and unleavened bread, offering blessings over the bread. Then, Jesus broke the bread and shared the cup of blessing as his own Body, Blood, Soul, and Divinity. I understood the significance—that Jesus was becoming the sacrificial lamb of God, atoning for their sins. Jesus commanded them to do the same in remembrance of him.

With the fourth cup, the Cup of Praise, absent, I listened attentively as the disciples began to sing the Hallel Psalms. The melody of Psalm 115 resonated in the air, bringing tears to my eyes. I understood that my nephew, Jesus, would soon make the ultimate sacrifice for the sins of humanity.

Then came the words of Psalm 116, describing how God hears our pleas for mercy. I recognized the importance of prayer and how it connected people to God. It reminded me of the strength Jesus found in prayer and the comfort it brought him.

As the disciples continued to sing, I heard the prophetic words of Psalm 118. The rejected stone becoming the cornerstone spoke directly of Jesus, destined to be rejected by religious leaders and the people. But

I also grasped that Jesus would become the foundation upon which the Christian faith would be built.

The Hallel Psalms infused my sister-in-law Mary's heart with calm, even amidst the impending torture and death of her son. I recognized that Jesus' sacrifice was part of God's grand plan, bringing salvation to humanity. As the disciples finished singing, I felt an overwhelming gratitude for my nephew and the message he brought to the world.

As the meal drew to a close and Jesus and the disciples departed for the Mount of Olives in the cover of darkness, a sense of peace settled over me. I knew that my nephew's mission was reaching its climax, and I was filled with awe and wonder at the perfect timing of it all. I understood that Jesus was the one who had come to save the world, and he would do so in his own way and at his own appointed time.

Judgement

Our prayer continued for Jesus to remain strong until His mission was complete. We knew we should get to the Praetorium where Pontius Pilate would declare the sentence on Jesus. The steep steps back down the hill slowed down our path back across the Kidron Valley and back up to the Golden Gate.

My wife Mary and I stood in the packed Praetorium Courtyard, our hearts heavy with grief and fear. My eyes scanned the crowd, looking for familiar faces among Jesus' followers, but all I saw were strangers. The rising morning sun burned fiercely down on us and making the air hot and dry. I wiped the sweat from my forehead, my eyes never leaving my nephew, who stood before the steps to Pilate's throne, surrounded by soldiers.

The sounds around me were chaotic. The murmurs of the crowd grew louder with every passing moment, and I could hear the clanking of armor and weapons as the soldiers moved around Jesus. The shouts of the soldiers as they barked orders to the people around them echoed in my ears. The whispers of the Pharisees and the Sadducees, who had plotted against Jesus for so long, reached my ears. They were working the crowd, trying to secure a sentence of death by crucifixion.

My eyes opened wide as I saw Jesus being pushed and pulled by the soldiers. They taunted Him, laughed at Him, and even spat on Him. My heart broke as I witnessed the bruises on His face, the blood trickling down His cheek from where one of the soldiers had struck Him. I felt a surge of anger and helplessness, wanting to rush forward and protect Him, to take Him in my arms and shield Him from the cruelty of the soldiers. But I knew I had to stay strong, to watch as my nephew face His accusers and be judged.

The sight before me was a nightmare. Jesus, the man I had come to know and love, was being accused of blasphemy, and I knew the penalty was severe. I listened as the high priest answered Pilate's questions, watched as Jesus remained silent, knowing that He had done nothing wrong. Fear was evident in His eyes, uncertainty about what was to come.

The trial seemed to drag on for hours, and I watched in silence. The jeers of the crowd grew louder, the Pharisees and Sadducees whispered among themselves, plotting against Jesus. They sought a way to condemn Him to death.

As the trial came to an end, a heavy weight settled in my heart. Jesus had been found guilty, condemned to death by crucifixion. I could hear the cheers of the crowd, the soldiers laughing and joking as they prepared to take Him away. I wanted to scream, to protest, but deep down, I knew it would be futile. Jesus had been judged, and there was nothing I could do to save Him.

Pontius Pilate, the Roman governor of Judea, ordered Jesus to be scourged as a form of punishment before deciding His fate. We believe Pilate hoped that the brutal beating would satisfy the bloodlust of the religious leaders who sought Jesus' execution, and perhaps even persuade them to spare His life.

I watched in horror as they stripped my nephew, tied Him to a post, and scourged Him mercilessly. The sickening sound of the whip striking His flesh reverberated through the air, each blow leaving behind a trail of blood and torn skin. The stench of sweat, fear, and blood filled my nostrils, mingling with the sounds of the soldiers' shouts and the gasps and cries of onlookers.

With every strike of the whip, with every scream of agony that escaped Jesus' lips, my heart broke a little more. How could they do this to Him? He had healed the sick, given sight to the blind, and preached love and forgiveness. Yet here He was, being beaten and humiliated, all because of the fear and jealousy of those in power. After most of the strikes, Jesus looked upward as He was telling His father, to let it happen, that it was the only way to defeat satan.

I fought back tears as Jesus was untied and handed His garments. His body was battered and bruised, barely recognizable. The soldiers mocked Him, placing a crown of thorns upon His head and a reed in His hand, pretending to pay homage to the "King of the Jews." The irony was not lost on me, but the sight filled me with anger and sadness.

Jesus was then led away, carrying His cross, towards the place of His execution. I followed behind, my footsteps heavy with sorrow. The journey to Golgotha was long and arduous, the weight of the cross bearing down on Jesus' battered body. He stumbled and fell several times, each time rising again with determination and resilience.

The crowd that lined the streets seemed to revel in His suffering, shouting insults and curses at Him. Some spat at Him, while others simply looked on with cold indifference. My heart ached as I witnessed the pain and humiliation He endured, yet He remained steadfast, focused on His mission.

Finally, we reached Golgotha, the place of the skull. Jesus was laid upon the cross, His hands and feet pierced with nails. The sound of the hammer striking against the metal echoed in my ears, a haunting reminder of the brutality of His crucifixion. I stood there, unable to tear my eyes away from the sight before me.

As the cross was lifted, a wave of agony washed over Jesus' face. His body trembled; His breath labored. The weight of the world's sins bore down on Him, and I could see the pain etched in every line of His face. His eyes met mine for a brief moment, and in that gaze, I saw love, forgiveness, and a profound sadness.

Time seemed to stand still as I watched my nephew hang upon that cross, His life slowly ebbing away. The sky drew dark, the air heavy with grief. The ground shook beneath our feet, as if even nature itself mourned the loss of this extraordinary man. I fell to my knees, tears streaming down my face, as I whispered a prayer for His suffering to end.

Mary motioned for me to draw near, that my sister-in-law, Mary, the Mother of God really needed me. Poor John had stayed up at the cross, consoling Her, but he was to overcome with his own grief. Then, Jesus uttered his final words, "It is finished," and with that, He breathed His last. The world grew silent, as if holding its breath in the wake of such a profound sacrifice. The weight of His death pressed upon me, an unbearable burden of sorrow and loss.

In that moment, I knew that everything had changed. The world would never be the same without Jesus. His love, His teachings, His sacrifice would resonate throughout history, forever transforming the lives of those who believed in Him.

As I stood there, still and broken myself, I vowed to carry His message forward, to share His story with the world. Jesus, my nephew, my friend, had shown me the way of love, of compassion, and of selflessness. Though He was gone, His spirit would live on, guiding me and countless others along the path of righteousness.

In the Shadow of Doubt

It was in the Upper Room, surrounded by the weight of despair and disbelief, that I sat quietly with my wife Mary. We felt isolated, cut off not only from the other disciples but also from the hope that once blazed within us. Whispers and tears filled the room, yet we remained lost in our own thoughts, the silence mirroring the deep sadness that engulfed us.

Mary leaned her weary head against my shoulder, seeking solace in my presence. Her eyes were swollen from ceaseless weeping, and her body bore the exhaustion of grief, both physical and emotional. I gently placed my arm around her, offering what little comfort I could muster.

"Mary," I spoke softly, my voice tinged with sorrow, "we have seen so much, heard His words of promise, and witnessed His miracles. How could it all end like this?"

Her voice trembled as she responded, doubt lacing her tone. "I don't know, Cleopas. I don't understand any of it. How could the Messiah, the Son of God, be taken from us? And how can we believe in His resurrection when our hearts lie shattered?"

A sigh escaped my lips as doubts gnawed at my own soul. "I, too, wrestle with these questions, Mary. The promises Jesus made, the hope He ignited within us—they all seem so distant now. We saw Him crucified; His body laid to rest in that tomb. How can we reconcile this with the hope of His resurrection?"

Across the room, my sister-in-law, the Blessed Mother Mary, sat with a face marked by profound sorrow. Our gazes briefly met, and in her eyes, I saw the reflection of my own doubts. She had borne witness to her son's crucifixion, standing strong amidst unimaginable pain. Yet even her faith seemed strained now.

"I remember when Jesus spoke of His impending death," Mary whispered, her voice quivering. "But He also said He would rise on the third day. We clung to those words, Cleopas, hoping against hope. Now, it feels like all we have left are shattered dreams."

I held Mary tighter, tears threatening to spill over. "Yes, Mary. We believed in Him with all our hearts. We saw Him heal the sick, raise the dead, and transform lives. But now, our faith wavers in the face of this tragedy. How can we trust that His promises were not in vain?"

Exhaustion deepened within Mary, casting a heavier shadow upon her spirit. "I am so tired, Cleopas. Physically, emotionally, and spiritually exhausted. I long for the strength to keep believing, to hold onto the glimmer of hope. But in this darkness, it becomes increasingly difficult."

I nodded; my voice heavy with grief. "I know, Mary. We must find a way to cling to what we have known, even when it seems impossible. We have seen miracles, experienced the power of His love. We must remember that, even now."

Our eyes met, conveying shared pain and vulnerability. I reached for Mary's hands, seeking unity amidst our doubts. "Let us draw strength from one another, Mary. We may not understand everything, but together, we can endure this darkness. We can carry each other's burdens, as He taught us to."

Glimmers of hope flickered in Mary's tired eyes. "Yes, Cleopas. Let us lean on one another, and let us also seek solace in His mother, who sits there, bearing a mother's anguish. She has known suffering, and perhaps she can help us find our way through this desolation."

We turned our gaze to the Blessed Mother, her presence emanating both resilience and sorrow. She had borne the weight of witnessing her own son's death, yet her faith remained unwavering. In her, I found a beacon of hope, a reminder that even amidst our doubts, our faith had a place to rest.

As we continued to sit together, Mary and I felt a flicker of hope reigniting within us. The road ahead would be difficult, and our doubts would not easily vanish. Yet, with each passing moment, our shared vulnerability and the presence of the Blessed Mother brought reassurance.

In the Upper Room, Mary and I found solace in our shared sorrow, knowing that our doubts and struggles were not borne alone. And as we awaited what lay beyond the third day, we discovered that even in the face of darkness, love and faith had the power to guide us through our deepest doubts and pain.

Through it all, we would walk hand in hand, leaning on one another, drawing strength from our shared journey and the memories of the miracles we had witnessed. And in the embrace of the Blessed Mother's unwavering faith, we would find the courage to hold on to the promises of resurrection, even in the shadow of doubt.

The Dawn of the Third Day

The morning of the third day dawned, casting a gentle glow upon the city. I found myself seated alongside my wife, Mary, in the Upper Room, surrounded by a haze of anticipation and uncertainty. The promise of resurrection lingered in the air, intermingling with the scent of the perfumes and oils the women had prepared to anoint the body of our beloved Jesus.

Mary held tightly onto the containers of perfumed ointments, her fingers tracing the delicate curves as if seeking solace in their touch. Her eyes mirrored the mixture of hope and trepidation that churned within my own soul. We sat in silence, the weight of our grief and doubts pressing upon us.

As the hours slipped away, an undercurrent of tension wove through the Upper Room. Suddenly, the door burst open, and the women hurriedly entered, their faces etched with confusion and disbelief. Their breathless voices struggled to convey the unimaginable truth.

"His body, it's not there," one of the women stammered, her voice trembling. "We don't know where they have taken Him."

In that moment, a profound stillness settled upon the room. The air grew heavy with the weight of uncertainty, and all eyes turned towards Peter and John, who exchanged a resolute glance. Without a word, they hastily departed, their footsteps echoing down the corridors as they sought answers.

Left in the wake of their departure, Mary and I exchanged worried glances. Doubt crept into our hearts, threatening to overshadow the flickering flame of hope that had burned within us. The room seemed to hold its breath as we grappled with the puzzling void left by the absence of Jesus's body.

Questions swirled through my mind. Had someone stolen His body? Or could it be that the incredible had transpired—a resurrection from the dead? The uncertainty gnawed at my soul, stirring a tempest of conflicting emotions. We had seen Him bring back to life the little girl, and even Lazarus after 3 days in the tomb, but how could He do it for Himself, from the grave?

As we sat in the Upper Room, the passage of time became both fluid and stagnant, as if eternity had taken hold of those fleeting moments. The hushed whispers and anxious glances exchanged among the disciples reflected the collective struggle we faced.

Hours stretched into an agonizing eternity, each minute an echo of the uncertainty that gripped our hearts. The silence was broken only by the distant sounds of the bustling city and the rhythmic beating of our own troubled breaths.

Finally, the heavy footsteps of Peter and John reverberated through the Upper Room, their faces etched with a blend of astonishment and bewilderment. As they entered, their words tumbled forth, carrying the weight of revelation.

"The tomb was empty," Peter exclaimed, his voice filled with awe. "We have seen for ourselves, Cleopas. His body was not there."

A profound mixture of relief, awe, and incredulity flooded the room. Hope rekindled within us, casting a radiant light upon the shadows of doubt. Could it be true? Had Jesus indeed conquered death, fulfilling His promise of resurrection?

As the news spread among us, the Upper Room erupted with a symphony of joy and wonder. Laughter mingled with tears, and the heavy burden of grief began to lift. The very air seemed to shimmer with the presence of the risen Christ.

Seeking Answers Amidst the Scorching Sun

The sun burned high in the sky, its scorching rays descending upon the parched land as my wife Mary and I set off on their journey. Our hearts heavy with sorrow and uncertainty, we had made the decision to leave Jerusalem and return to our farm in Emmaus, unable to bear the weight of not knowing what had become of their nephew Jesus's body.

The walk would take us approximately two hours, and as we ventured forth, the dusty road stretched out before us, shimmering under the relentless sun. The heat bore down upon us, intensifying the turmoil within our hearts. We wondered how, a few days earlier in the mid-day sun, Jesus was able to carry that heavy cross after being beaten and flogged for hours. With each step we took, our conversation echoed our growing concern.

"Why would anyone do such a thing?" Mary asked, her voice filled with both frustration and sadness. "To steal Jesus's body? It seems unimaginable."

I nodded, wiping the sweat from my brow with the back of my hand. The warmth of the day only served to heighten our distress, the physical discomfort mirroring the turmoil of our emotions.

"I can't fathom the motives behind such an act," I replied, my voice tinged with a mixture of anger and confusion. "But we cannot let our doubts consume us. We must remain steadfast in our faith, even in the face of this bewildering turn of events."

As we continued their walk, the rhythmic crunch of gravel beneath our feet scattered our conversation. Each step seemed to magnify the weight of uncertainty that rested upon our shoulders. Even though we'd travelled this road many times, the road ahead appeared to stretch endlessly, mirroring the expanse of our doubts and fears.

The silence between us grew, a testament to the depths of their introspection. Thoughts tumbled through my mind, like leaves caught in a gust of wind. Why would someone go to such lengths to steal Jesus's body? What purpose could it possibly serve?

Our nephew had been a man of compassion and healing, a beacon of hope in a world shadowed by despair. His teachings had challenged convention, his miracles had inspired awe. But his crucifixion had shattered our hopes, leaving us grappling with the enormity of our loss.

Yet, amidst the confusion and despair, Mary and I clung to the flickering ember of faith that still burned within them. Though it wavered, threatened by the gusts of doubt, we refused to let it be extinguished.

As the minutes turned into an hour, our conversation shifted. We began to recount the moments spent with Jesus as a child then a young man, the miracles we had witnessed, and the teachings that had stirred our souls. I thought about how much joy that my brother Joseph would have had seeing Jesus grow to be the man we had the privilege to see grow. The memories brought both solace and pain, as we struggled to reconcile the promise of resurrection with the reality we faced.

With each passing minute, the sun's relentless rays intensified, scorching the earth and sapping our strength. The physical discomfort became a metaphor for the doubts and fears that plagued us. We trudged onward; our determination unwavering.

As the journey neared its midpoint, Mary and I found solace in the familiarity of the path. The sights and sounds of the countryside evoked memories of simpler times, of toiling in the fields, and finding solace in the embrace of our humble farm.

And so, with the sun casting longer shadows behind us, Mary and I continued our trek toward Emmaus, our hearts burdened by unanswered questions, our steps guided by a glimmer of hope. Little did we know that our journey held the potential to change our lives forever!

This Man Hasn't a Clue

As we neared a peak in the path, we were greeted by a man coming from the direction of Abu Ghosh. Like most of us on the path, this man had a long walking stick, but his seemed to have a bend that seemed to have been worked for many days of soaking the end in warm water and then bending it around a couple of heavy rocks only enough to gently form the curvature without it snapping while it dried. This took many days to form, especially because it was the larger end of the stick. Joseph made so many of these for the Shepherds, the hook to guide the sheep along the path and the heavy end to fight off the evil ones after his sheep.

We were confused that this man had not only a walking stick, but one with a shepherd's hook, yet he walked alone, without his flock. Mary complimented the man for the details which appeared in the stick after she wiped the tears away from her eyes. She said, "you must be a shepherd, but where is your flock?"

The man giggled and said they are all over this land. He continued, "many have scattered, but they will return to me when I call for them". Mary asked him if he made the stick himself. Again, he giggled and said, "I can do a lot of things, but the wood itself came from a tree up north." The snarky comment first felt disrespectful, but when we all laughed, we all knew that God the Father had put this man in our path to lift our spirits. The man then said, "I am sorry to be joking at a time it seemed like you both were grieving about something". He then said, "I traded some freshly lamb meat for this stick with a real craftsman in Nazareth. He was a wonderful and honest man, a true craftsman." He said that he has been working on it for many years and knew eventually he would find just the right person to give it to.

Mary and I looked at each other and smiled in amazement. Could this be a coincidence? I thought, it must be, as I am sure I have never met this man before who was walking with us now.

Mary said to the man, "yes, we are very distraught. Our nephew spent the last 3 years of life trying to share with others to love God with all your heart, to love others, even if they hate you and to serve each other as a sign of your love for God." She continued, "I'm surprised you haven't heard of him; He is Jesus of Nazareth. They beat him and nailed him to a tree and left him to die". Then she told him he had to be the only one to not know that this happened.

The man said, "I know this man, Jesus. I have studied every scroll ever written. I know exactly why He came from the Father when He did, why He did what He did and why He did it at this exact time". He asked if her could share all that he knew, and we quickly said "Yes, of course – please do".

Little did they know that their companion on this journey was none other than Jesus Himself. He had risen from the dead, victorious over sin and death, but His appearance was disguised to them, for their eyes were kept from recognizing Him. Jesus, the author of salvation history, longed to reveal the depths of God's love to them, to unfold the plan that had been set in motion since before the beginning of time.

With compassion in His voice, He began to speak, weaving a tapestry of truth and revelation before our bewildered eyes.

My dear friends, let me share with you the story of love and redemption that started in the heart of God the Father Himself. Before the foundation of the world, God conceived a plan—a plan born out of His infinite love for humanity, His image-bearers. He created the universe, the earth, and all that is in it, as a stage for this divine drama to unfold.

It was an infinite and boundless love that emanated from the very heart of God the Father. He looked upon His creation and saw the crowning jewel of His handiwork, humanity. We were made in His image and likeness, destined for a relationship of intimate communion with our Creator.

But within this grand design, there emerged an enemy, a fallen angel named Satan, who sought to mar God's masterpiece. He aimed to destroy humanity, to separate them from their Creator and plunge them into darkness. This adversary understood the power of sin, the separation it could cause between God and His beloved children. Separation and the sense of bondage would be the only way evil would win. Yet, even in the face of this rebellion, God would not abandon very beings God cherished so deeply. Instead, He equipped us with knowledge of this enemy and how to engage in spiritual warfare, to resist the powers that seek to enslave us.

Out of His true love, God knew that something had to be done. He desired to rescue humanity from the dire consequences of sin and restore the broken relationship between Himself and His creation. From the moment sin tainted the pristine beauty of creation, God the Father, in His infinite wisdom and boundless love, set in motion a plan that would ultimately bring redemption to His beloved children. This plan, intricately woven through the pages of the Old Testament, reveals the profound depths of God's desire for reconciliation and restoration.

Our journey home to Emmaus continued, Mary and I hanging onto every word spoken by the stranger walking beside us. I can't explain it, but there was something captivating about His presence, something that stirred our hearts and ignited a glimmer of hope within us.

He continued, Before the beginning of time, the Father knew the power of sin and the devastating consequences it would unleash upon humanity. Yet, in His perfect love, He refused to abandon us to our fate. He desired to rescue us from the bondage of sin, to mend the shattered relationship between Himself and His creation.

Throughout the scrolls of the Scripture, there are glimpses, foreshadowing of the coming Savior. In the book of Genesis, the first chapters tell the story of our origin and the tragic fall of humanity. Adam and Eve, your first parents, yielded to the serpent's cunning deception and chose to disobey God's command. This act of disobedience ushered in sin and death, leading the human race into bondage. But even in the midst of this despair, God's plan for redemption began to take shape. From the moment sin entered the world immediately after the fall of Adam and Eve, God the Father proclaimed that the seed of the woman, whom you know as Mary, would crush the head of the serpent (Genesis 3:15).

He continued, recounting the stories of Abraham, Moses, David, and the prophets, highlighting how each of their lives and experiences pointed to Jesus. Abraham, the father of many nations, believed in the promise of God, and it was credited to him as righteousness. Through his lineage, Jesus was born into the world. Moses, the deliverer of the Israelites from slavery in Egypt, foreshadowed the greater deliverance Jesus would bring through His sacrifice on the cross.

He made a covenant with Abraham, declaring that through his descendants, all nations would be blessed (Genesis 12:3). This covenant foreshadowed the universal scope of salvation, the widening embrace of God's love that would encompass all humanity through the person of the Messiah.

This somewhat cryptic prophecy foretold the coming of a Savior who would conquer the very enemy that sought to destroy humanity. It revealed God's unwavering commitment to rescue His children from the clutches of sin and death.

This Scripture serve as signposts, pointing to the divine purpose that would unfold in the fullness of time. Let's sit for a bit to rest and together, talk through what will be known as salvation history and uncover the some of the profound reasons behind God's plan for Jesus' incarnation. Jesus is the embodiment of God's love, the fulfillment of His plan. His purpose in coming to this world was not merely to perform miracles and teach moral values. No, He became human to personally rescue and redeem each individual, to creatively outwit Satan, the deceiver, and bring about the restoration of God's kingdom.

The sacrificial system established in the book of Exodus offered glimpses of the ultimate sacrifice that was to come. The blood of innocent animals served as a temporary covering for sin, but it pointed to a greater Lamb who would be offered as a perfect and final sacrifice (Exodus 12:21-28). This prefigured the necessity of Jesus' atoning death, the ultimate act of love that would cleanse humanity of its sins.

As for David, He continued, he was anointed as king of Israel, a ruler after God's own heart. Yet, even David recognized his need for a greater king, a Messiah who would reign forever. In the Psalms, he wrote, "The Lord says to my Lord: Sit at my right hand until I make your enemies a footstool for your feet." Those words were not merely spoken by David to one of his earthly descendants, but they were a prophecy, speaking of Jesus' eternal kingship.

He paused for a moment, reflecting on the ancient words that spoke of His arrival. Then, with great authority and tenderness, in the book of Isaiah, it is written, "Therefore, the Lord Himself will give you a sign: The virgin will conceive and give birth to a son, and will call him Immanuel." This child, born of a virgin, would be more than just a man. He would be God in the flesh, dwelling among His people, offering them the gift of salvation."

Mary and I listened with a mixture of awe and disbelief. The pieces of the puzzle were slowly falling into place, and yet, the veil still remained. We couldn't understand why they couldn't recognize the truth before their very eyes. But their hearts were opening to the truth, their faith growing with every word spoken by the stranger.

He could tell our hearts were ready for more, so He reminded us to not forget the prophet Isaiah, whose words held great significance. Isaiah spoke of a suffering servant, one who would bear the sins of the people, and by His wounds, they would be healed. In particular, in Isaiah 53, it is written, "He was pierced for our transgressions, He was crushed for our iniquities; the punishment that brought us peace was on Him, and by His wounds, we are healed."

These words speak of the very purpose for which Jesus came into the world—to lay down His life as a ransom for many, to offer salvation and healing to all who would believe.

Micah proclaimed that from Bethlehem, the city of David, a ruler would come forth whose origins were from old, from ancient times (Micah 5:2). These prophecies stirred the hearts of the faithful, instilling a longing for the fulfillment of God's promises.

In the fullness of time, when the world was ripe for His arrival, God sent forth His Son, born of a virgin, to dwell among humanity (Matthew 1:23). The eternal Word became flesh, and Jesus Christ, entered into this broken and sinful world. Jesus, fully God and fully man, embarked on a mission of rescue and redemption. His life, death, and resurrection were not mere acts of moral teaching or displays of power; they were the culmination of God's plan to save humanity.

As Jesus walked this land, He saw firsthand the effects of sin and the bondage it brought upon the human race. He witnessed the brokenness, the pain, and the despair that engulfed people's lives. But He also saw the flickering flames of hope, the longing for something greater, something beyond the reach of this fallen world.

You see, my dear friends, it was love that drove God to send Jesus into the world. It was love that compelled Him to give His only Son, that whoever believes in Him should not perish but have eternal life. God so loved the world, so loved each and every one of you, that He wanted to restore the broken relationship, to bring you back into communion with Him.

Jesus' purpose was clear—to rescue and save each individual, to ingeniously outfox Satan, the deceiver, and to bring about the restoration of God's kingdom. He came not to condemn but to offer salvation, to set the captives free. His love for humanity compelled Him to take on the form of a servant, to humble Himself and walk among you.

Through His life, Jesus revealed the heart of the Father. He taught of His love, His mercy, and His desire for reconciliation. He performed miracles, not as mere displays of power, but as signs of the breaking in of the kingdom of God. He healed the sick, raised the dead, and forgave sins, demonstrating the transformative power of God's grace.

The climax of this divine drama was reached on the cross. There, in the most profound act of sacrificial love the world has ever witnessed, He bore the weight of sin upon His shoulders. The sins of humanity, past, present, and future, were nailed to the tree. The forces of evil rejoiced, believing they had triumphed over the Son of God! Little did they understand the depth of the Father's love and the power of His plan. Ha!

But they could not comprehend the depth of God's love. For in the resurrection, everything changed. Death was defeated, sin was conquered, and a new creation was birthed. The victory He won on the cross echoed through the ages, reverberating with the power to transform lives and restore the broken relationship between God and humanity.

Through His death and resurrection, each individual who accepts the gift of salvation becomes a new creation. The old has passed away; behold, the new has come. This is not a mere metaphor, but a profound spiritual reality. The chains of sin are shattered, and a new life in communion with God is offered.

In the death of Jesus, He took upon Himself the weight of sin, the punishment that humanity deserved. He willingly bore the shame, the agony, and the separation from the Father, so that you might be reconciled to God. Through His sacrifice, the debt of sin was paid in full, and the power of sin and death was broken. The ransom was paid, slavery to sin emancipated and the evil one forfeited the lost sheep to the Great Shepherd.

Our hearts stirred with a profound mix of sorrow and awe. We scarcely comprehended the magnitude of the love that compelled Jesus to endure such suffering on their behalf. His words resonated within them, touching the depths of their souls and stirring a newfound hope.

But my dear friends, He continued with voice filled with triumph, the story does not end with His death. On the third day, Jesus conquered sin and death, bursting forth from the tomb in glorious resurrection. The victory He achieved through His resurrection changed everything. It was the ultimate confirmation that God's plan of redemption was accomplished, that the power of sin was defeated, and that eternal life was made available to all who believe.

Now, in response to this extraordinary news, each individual is called to a transformative journey of faith. Inwardly, we are invited to surrender our lives fully to Jesus Christ, acknowledging Him as Lord and Savior. We will continue to engage in worship, offering praise and thanksgiving to God for His immeasurable love. We are called to completely detach ourselves from the idols of this world, recognizing that true fulfillment can only be found in Him.

Outwardly, we now are commissioned to actively participate in the liberation and transformation of the world. We now become ambassadors of reconciliation, builders of God's kingdom in our relationships, communities, and institutions. We must reflect His love, mercy, and justice, bringing light to the darkest corners of society, thus continuing to focus the Light of Christ on the hiding and coward evil one.

This is the essence of the good news that will transcend time and space. It is a love story woven by the hands of the Father before the foundations of the world. It is a tapestry of redemption, restoration, and the recreation of His world. It is an invitation to join in this divine dance of grace, where each step taken in faith has the power to bring forth glimpses of heaven on earth.

So hear the call of love echoing through the ages. Embrace the gift of salvation, for in it lies the promise of a transformed life in communion with God and others. Step boldly into the divine story that began before time itself, and let your life be a testament to the redemptive power of God's love. Though the events of these past days may seem perplexing and discouraging, remember that they are part of the greater story of redemption. Trust in God's unfailing love and know that His plan is at work, even in the darkest of times.

A silence fell upon the three of us as they processed the weight of the revelation. Our hearts burned within us, our spirits stirred with a profound mix of hope and longing. As we entered Emmaus, Mary and I felt a warmth radiating from within. Though our eyes were still veiled, their hearts burned with a newfound hope. We listened intently, captivated by the words of this mysterious man who seemed to understand their deepest longings. Little did we know that this journey would be a pivotal moment in our lives, a divine encounter that would forever change their understanding of true love and redemption.

The man stopped at the gate and wished us well in our life's journey. The day had begun to fade, giving way to the soft glow of twilight and we knew He would be walking in the dark soon, so we invited Him to stay with us. We were so excited He said yes to our offer. We were anxious to ask Him how he knew the Scriptures and about Jesus so well.

The Breaking of the Bread

The sun sank low on the horizon, casting long shadows across the weary landscape of Emmaus. Mary and I walked alongside the stranger who had joined us on our journey from Jerusalem. We approached our humble dwelling, a small house nestled amidst the village, feeling a mixture of exhaustion and anticipation. Our hearts were heavy with grief, confusion, and a glimmer of hope as we had just returned from the city where Jesus had been crucified.

With each step, the weariness of the long and arduous journey weighed upon our bodies. The air was filled with a dust stirred up by our footsteps, mingled with the scent of wildflowers that adorned the countryside. As we reached the familiar wooden door, worn with age, anticipation mingled with our fatigue.

I grasped the iron latch, its rusted mechanism protesting with a soft groan as I opened the door. The door swung open, revealing the interior of our humble abode. The room was dimly lit by the sunlight passing thru our windows as it lowered toward the horizon. It casting shifting shadows on the rough stone walls as our neighbors passed by the windows as they returned from the fields. The space exuded a sense of warmth and familiarity, a sanctuary amidst the bustling world we had just come from.

We stepped inside, setting down our travel bags with a thud upon the earthen floor. A cloud of dust rose, carrying the earthly scent of home and the fragrance of dried herbs that hung from the rafters. Mary yelled at me for not setting them down more gently. I was exhausted and had done the same thing without Mary commenting, so it must have been because of our guest that she was so sensitive. The comforting aroma of cedarwood, aged and weathered, enveloped us, reminding us of the simplicity and solace we had left behind a little over a week earlier.

The hearth stood cold and dormant in the corner of the room, the remnants of previous fires now nothing more than ash. We would need to start a fire to ward off the evening chill that seeped through the walls. The faint scent of wood smoke in the air was not from our own hearth but likely from the neighboring homes, signaling the warmth and life that dwelled within this close-knit community.

As we moved further into the house, our footsteps muffled by the worn rugs, our eyes fell upon a modest wooden table placed against the far wall. It stood bare, waiting to be adorned with a simple meal—a loaf of bread, a jug of wine, and a few meager offerings of olives and dried figs. Hunger tugged at our weary bodies, reminding us of our physical needs after days of fasting and mourning.

And there, standing beside us, was the man who had accompanied us on our journey. Though we still did not know his true identity, his presence brought an unspoken comfort and a sense of solace. His eyes held a depth of compassion that touched the depths of our weary hearts, and we welcomed his companionship without hesitation.

The three of us gathered wood and kindling around the back of the house. It was so good to have this much younger man there to help collect and carry the wood. Here we are, Mary at 55 years old and me at 58 years old. Our guest must be at least 20 years our junior. Especially after our 7-mile hike, it was good to have him to do the heavy lifting!

As we walked back to the house, I mentioned that we never did ask him what his name was. He said he goes by many names, but most called him "Iam". I said, "Doesn't that mean right hand?" He said, "exactly! But my mom said it is a good name for someone with mental and emotional balance, although my dad says He likes the meaning of the 3 letters. The "I" means you are a compassionate person who feels things deeply. The "A" means that you are your own person, ambitious, freethinking and does not cave due to pressure from others. "M" means you are always on the go, not needing much sleep. I guess that fits me rather well!

Iam stacked the larger wood for use later and arranged the kindling over an old bird's nest we found that had fallen from a tree. Iam then started striking flint against stone to spark the first flicker of fire. The tiny flame grew, crackling and dancing as it consumed the dry timber. The room soon filled with the warmth and gentle glow of the hearth, casting soft shadows upon the worn furniture and the rugs that had seen years of use.

Iam and I set off the get some water as the fiery orange hues of the setting sun painted the sky, casting long shadows across the village towards the village well as if to show us the way. The air was thick with the warm scent of dusty earth, and a gentle breeze carried the distant sound of children's laughter, intermingling with the songs of birds returning to their nests. It was the perfect time to fetch water for our evening meal and cleaning.

The path to the well was a well-trodden one, lined with tall swaying grass and scattered wildflowers, their petals dancing in the fading light. The rhythmic crunch of our footsteps blended with the symphony of nature, creating a melody that soothed my weary soul. The day had been long, filled with emotion, and physical stress, and the thought of quenching our thirst with cool water rejuvenated my spirit.

As we approached the well, its ancient stone structure rose before us like a weathered monument to time itself. Moss clung to its sides, an intricate tapestry of green against the gray stone. Iam and I paused for a moment, taking in the sight, before setting our buckets down with a soft thud on the ground. The anticipation of the water's embrace heightened the intensity of the moment.

With the pulsing creak of the rusty pulley, I lowered the bucket into the darkness below, feeling its weight increase as it disappeared into the depths. A moment later, the bucket broke the surface, water cascading from it like liquid silver. Iam and I exchanged a glance, a silent agreement to continue our task, and he began filling the second bucket while I held onto the first.

The water was cool against my skin, a refreshing caress that seemed to wash away the weariness of the day. Droplets dripped from my fingers, mirroring the tears of joy that threatened to escape my eyes. It was in moments like these that I realized the simplicity and beauty of life, the interconnectedness of all things.

As Iam finished filling the second bucket, the weight of the water increased, testing our strength. With a grunt, we hoisted the buckets onto our shoulders, the burden reminding us of the importance of our task. The weight pressed against our bones, a constant reminder of the hardships endured by our ancestors.

With each step, the rhythmic sloshing of water resonated within our ears, a symphony of sustenance that harmonized with the beating of our hearts. The path home seemed longer, as if nature itself conspired to prolong our journey and deepen our appreciation for the gift we carried. The sunset's glow dimmed, replaced by the soft shimmer of moonlight casting ghostly shadows upon the ground.

The village came into view, its humble huts and bustling market square a testament to the resilience of its people. We were welcomed by the sound of crackling fires and the aroma of spices mingling with the warm scent of freshly baked bread. The villagers busied themselves with their evening routines, oblivious to the invisible thread that connected us all.

We reached our destination, our arms trembling with the strain of carrying the water. With a sigh of relief, we poured the contents of the buckets into the designated vessels, the water finding its rightful place. A sense of accomplishment washed over us, like the blood flowing through our veins, reminding us that even the simplest of tasks held immense importance.

The night settled in around us, a comforting blanket that embraced us with its cool embrace. Iam and I shared a silent moment, appreciating the beauty and tranquility that surrounded us. The journey to the well had not only quenched our physical thirst but also nourished our souls, reminding us of the interconnectedness of all life and the resilience of the human spirit.

And as the night stretched on, I couldn't help but marvel at the profound simplicity of our existence, finding solace in the ritual of fetching water from the well. It was in these timeless moments that the weight of the world seemed to lift, replaced by a profound connection to the land, the people, and the eternal cycle of life.

We placed our tired bodies around the table. The gentle flicker of candlelight danced upon our faces, casting an ethereal glow that seemed to mirror the growing intensity of their souls.

Iam began to speak once more, his voice infused with a type of divine authority that resonated deep within our beings. "Dear friends, as we continue on this journey of unveiling the depths of God's plan, let us delve further into the significance of His death and resurrection."

The stranger arranged the wine and bread in front of him picked up the bread and began a prayer that sounded so warm. He began breaking the bread and handed pieces to each of us and pouring the wine. As we partook in this simple act, a sense of wonder enveloped us. The stranger's words carried a weight of wisdom and understanding that resonated with the deepest parts of our beings. There was a familiarity in his voice, as if he had been with us all along, guiding and comforting us through our darkest moments.

And then, as he commanded us to take these and eat and drink, for these are His true Body and true Blood, shed for the sins of all. Our eyes immediately were opened to the truth! The stranger, this companion who had walked with us on our journey, was Jesus himself—the very one we had mourned and believed to be lost forever.

It was his resurrected presence that filled the room, radiating a profound sense of love and redemption.

In that moment, exhaustion and anticipation mingled within us. We were weary from the journey, physically and emotionally drained, yet a renewed sense of hope sparked within our hearts. The arrival of Jesus in our home, the breaking of bread and the sharing of wine, marked a new beginning—a journey of faith and understanding that would carry us forward with renewed strength and purpose.

Suddenly, Jesus, vanished from our sight. As quickly as he appeared on the road, He left our sight with the same speed. Mary and I immediately recalled portions of the discussions he talked about on the road – about how excited that Elizabeth was caught off guard by the Blessed Mother Mary when She visited her in Ein Karem with the baby Jesus in Her womb, how the disciples were out in the boat in a storm threatening to capsize the boat and Jesus suddenly appeared, along with many other examples of how He seemed to always appear out of no where to those who love him are afraid or worried how they can make it another moment, another day.

Our minds raced with the realization that they had been walking alongside the very fulfillment of prophecies. The promised Messiah stood right beside them, sharing the mysteries of God's plan. Though their eyes were still unable to perceive the truth, their spirits were stirred with a growing sense of awe and wonder.

Overwhelmed by a sense of expectancy, we eagerly agreed, our hearts burning within us for the revelation that had been shared with us on the road. With a sense of urgency to share with the others about our walk to Emmaus, as the sun set and darkness embraced the land, we set our sights on Jerusalem and ran all the way up the hill, seven miles!

Fill and Light the Lamps - You are Going to Want to Hear This!

We ran all the way to the bottom of the steps! Our excitement overflowed to give us the strength to run all the way back after such a long day, but we had to tell them. Andrew was guarding the door at the top of the steps and quickly ran down to our aid. He yelled for Mary of Magdala to fetch us some water.

They were all eager to hear why we returned so quickly. We began to share the news of our walk to Emmaus, meeting a stranger along the way and learning that it was the risen Lord! Mary said that about 6 miles of the trip we walked along side this man whose identity was hidden from us all afternoon.

I chimed in and said "This man met up with us as we descended from Jerusalem yet said that he had not heard the news about Jesus", then He asked us how special Jesus was to us and our friends. We told him that He had followers for 3 years, travelling with Him throughout Idumea, Judea, Samaria, Galilee, Trachonitis, Decapolis and Perea. We told him that we were His aunt and uncle, and that His mother, Mary, was the closest of the disciples.

We told him that Jesus was a true scholar of the scriptures, how He could quote anything from the scrolls from Genesis to Malachi and be totally correct, even with a deep understanding of the meaning. The stranger said that he also prided himself on the inspired word of God in the scrolls.

He paused for a moment, allowing the weight of his words to sink in. Then, with unwavering certainty, he continued, "In the book of

Genesis, we see the consequences of humanity's fall, the entanglement of sin that held the human race captive. The bondage of sin was a weight too heavy for you to bear on your own, for it separated you from the love and presence of God."

"But in God's infinite love and wisdom, He conceived a plan to rescue you from this bondage, to restore the broken relationship between God and humanity. And that plan, my dear friends, involved the incarnation of Jesus, His death on the cross, and the ultimate victory of His resurrection."

Our hearts began to hang on every word, we listened intently as this stranger unbelievably wove together the threads of salvation history for us! He spoke of the sacrifice of the Passover lamb, which prefigured Jesus' own sacrifice, the Lamb of God who takes away the sins of the world. He spoke of the foreshadowing prophecies that pointed to Jesus' crucifixion, the piercing of his hands and feet, and the pouring out of his blood.

We were baffled as to how this stranger suddenly knew so much about the recent events from Jerusalem. Perhaps he was one of the bystanders who followed Jesus from a distance, but never got so close to become a true follower of Jesus?

As the stranger spoke of Jesus' resurrection, a glimmer of recognition began to stir within our hearts but he didn't look familiar or sound like anyone we knew. We remembered the reports from this morning of the empty tomb, the testimonies of the women who had encountered the angels. Could this stranger be one of the angels walking with us?

With a mix of trepidation and hope, I mustered the courage to ask the stranger, "Sir, we have listened to your words with captivated attention. They have stirred our hearts and ignited a fire within us. But we cannot help but wonder... Who are you? Your words carry a divine authority, and they resonate deep within us."

The stranger turned to us, his eyes full of compassion and love. With a gentle smile, he revealed, "My dear friends, I am a traveler with no place to lay my head. I have seen you in the crowds and have witnessed everything that Jesus has done and everything you and the others have done for Him and His Mother. I am very aware of the depths of God's plan with you."

Overwhelmed by the weight and confusion of the encounter, we asked him to continue. I only wished we would have had written these discussions down and you would hear the details he shared.

The main theme he shared with us was the concept of the battle between good and evil. He said is has been a common theme in religious and philosophical discussions for ages. These examples illustrate how God intervened in specific situations to ensure His purposes were fulfilled, overcoming evil and demonstrating His power, wisdom, and faithfulness.

It hurt the Father when satan left heaven and brought with him one third of the other angels. The Father allowed them to go and allowed mankind to have free will – to choose to follow goodness or to choose selfishness, sin as did the evil one. Ever since, the evil one has thought he could win a battle for the souls the vulnerable by forcing God to take away free will to save them. But, according to this stranger, God never has.

I said, "Let's see... what else did he tell us Mary"?

She said, "Cleopas, it was just about 7 hours ago! But where to start. Hmm, He explained the story of Noah and the Great Flood: In Genesis, the evil and corruption of humanity grieved God, and He decided to bring a flood to cleanse the earth. However, God found favor in Noah, a righteous man, and chose him to build an ark to save himself, his family, and representatives of all living creatures. Through Noah's obedience and trust in God's instructions, humanity was preserved, and a new beginning was made possible after the floodwaters receded. Throughout the generations we have to remember to show obedience to God and always trust in His commands."

I said, "and we all know the story about Joseph, the son of Jacob, was sold into slavery by his jealous brothers. He was taken to Egypt, where he faced numerous trials and temptations. However, God was with Joseph and granted him wisdom, enabling him to interpret dreams. Through his God-given gift, Joseph became a trusted advisor to Pharaoh and helped save Egypt and surrounding nations from a severe famine. In doing so, Joseph also reunited with his family and brought about reconciliation. We will always face trials, but the stranger explained that God will give gifts to those who do not complain about the trials He allows."

"And The Israelites were enslaved in Egypt for generations. But God raised up Moses as their deliverer and sent him to confront Pharaoh with the demand to let the people go. Despite Pharaoh's resistance, God performed mighty signs and wonders, known as the ten plagues, demonstrating His power over the gods of Egypt. Eventually, Pharaoh relented, and the Israelites were freed, leading to their journey towards the Promised Land. Imagine if Moses felt the call of God, but failed to act on it"?

Then Mary spoke up again, "The Philistine giant Goliath posed a great threat to the Israelites, mocking and defying the army of God. David, a young shepherd boy, faced Goliath with faith in God and defeated him with a single stone from his slingshot. This unexpected victory showcased God's power working through a seemingly insignificant individual, demonstrating that He can overcome any obstacle."

I asked for another cup of water, then said "These examples highlight instances where God intervened to counteract the plans of evil and bring about His Own purposes. There are numerous other accounts that reveal God's sovereignty, wisdom, and redemptive plan in the face of evil and adversity.

For example, "The Battle of Jericho - The city of Jericho was a fortified stronghold that posed a significant obstacle for the Israelites as they entered the Promised Land. God instructed Joshua, the leader of Israel, to march around the city for seven days, and on the seventh day, the walls of Jericho miraculously collapsed, leading to Israel's victory. We all were just at Jericho, it's a huge city to walk across, much less around! Ponder the problems if Joshua refused to do as requested"!

Mary then recalled another brave and obedient servant, "When the evil Haman sought to annihilate the Jewish people in ancient Persia, God raised up Esther, a Jewish queen, to intervene. Through Esther's bravery and wisdom, she exposed Haman's plot to King Xerxes, leading to the salvation of her people."

"Daniel remained faithful to God despite a decree forbidding prayer to anyone other than King Darius. As a result, he was thrown into a den of lions. However, God protected Daniel, and he emerged unharmed. This demonstrated God's power over earthly rulers and His faithfulness to His followers.", I said

I continued, "Of course, the crucifixion of Jesus initially seemed like a victory for evil forces. However, through His resurrection, Jesus defeated sin and death, providing salvation and hope to all who believe in Him. Imagine how satan's party came to an abrupt end when Jesus rose from the dead!".

Everyone laughed! It seemed good to be on the winning side and begin to laugh a bit. But the best joy was yet to come!

We said that there were many other things that the stranger told us as we walked to Emmaus. But the best part was when we reclined at the table for our evening meal, just a couple hours ago. I said, "the stranger picked up the Bread, gave thanks to God, then said 'Take this, for this is My Body'. Our hearts melted right then – for we knew at that moment, It was Jesus!!! Jesus Christ Is Risen! He is Risen Indeed!"

Don't miss out!

Visit the website below and you can sign up to receive emails whenever John H Brennan publishes a new book. There's no charge and no obligation.

https://books2read.com/r/B-A-KVCX-TJTKC

Also by John H Brennan

Thru The First Disciple's Eyes
Thru the First Disciple's Eyes
Through the Eyes of the Disciple Jesus Loved
Through the Eyes of Cleopas

Standalone
Advice From Above
The Rosary Revealed

About the Author

John lives in upstate NY with his beautiful wife of over 40 years, Theresa. We are blessed to have all of our children and grandchildren nearby, even though 2 grandchildren are on the nearby part of Heaven, showering us with prayers through Jesus.